Operational Guidance to Local Authorities:
Parking Policy and Enforcement

Traffic Management Act 2004

March 2008

London: TSO

TSO
information & publishing solutions

Published by TSO (The Stationery Office) and available from:

Online
www.tsoshop.co.uk

Mail, Telephone, Fax & E-mail
TSO
PO Box 29, Norwich NR3 1GN
Telephone orders/General enquiries: 0870 6005522
Fax orders: 0870 6005533
E-mail: customer.services@tso.co.uk
Textphone: 0870 240 3701

TSO Shops
16 Arthur Street, Belfast BT1 4GD
028 9023 8451
Fax 028 9023 5401
71 Lothian Road, Edinburgh EH3 9AZ
0870 606 5566
Fax 0870 606 5588

TSO@Blackwell and other Accredited Agents

Department for Transport
Great Minster House
76 Marsham Street
London SW1P 4DR
Telephone 020 7944 8300

Web site www.dft.gov.uk

© Crown copyright 2008

Copyright in the typographical arrangement rests with the Crown.

This publication, excluding logos, may be reproduced free of charge in any format or medium for non-commercial research, private study or for internal circulation within an organisation. This is subject to it being reproduced accurately and not used in a misleading context. The copyright source of the material must be acknowledged and the title of the publication specified.

For any other use of this material, apply for a Click-Use Licence at www.opsi.gov.uk/click-use/index.htm, or by writing to the Licensing Division, Office of Public Sector Information, St Clements House, 2–16 Colegate, Norwich NR3 1BQ, fax 01603 723000, e-mail licensing@opsi.x.gsi.gov.uk

This is a value added publication which falls outside the scope of the Public Sector Information Click-Use Licence.

ISBN 978 0 11 552943 6

Second impression with minor amendments May 2008

Printed in Great Britain on paper containing at least 75% recycled fibre.

Contents

1	**Introduction**	7
2	**The policy context**	9
	National policy	9
	Local policy	10
	Parking provision	11
3	**Objectives of civil enforcement**	13
	Policy objectives	13
	CPE financial objectives	14
4	**Appraising, ensuring the effectiveness of and reporting on civil parking enforcement**	16
	Appraising CPE	16
	Ensuring the effectiveness of CPE	17
	Reporting	18
	Parking Annual Reports: possible contents	20
	Financial	20
	Statistical	20
	Performance against targets	21
	Financial reporting	21
	Returns to Government on enforcement action	22
5	**Consultation and communication with the public**	23
	Consultation	23
	Communication	24
	Content of parking communications	25
6	**Training and professionalism in civil parking enforcement**	27
	Back office and management staff	28
	Civil Enforcement Officers (CEOs)	28
	CEO duties	29
	Discretion	31
	Training	31
	Probation	34
	Camera operators	34
	Immobilisation and removal teams	34

7	**Choice and certification of devices for camera enforcement**	36
	Devices certified by the Secretary of State	36
	Procedures for operating parking enforcement systems	37
8	**Enforcement**	38
	Civil Enforcement Officers' handbook	38
	Uniforms	38
	Equipment	39
	Hand-held computers	39
	Mobile communications	40
	Digital cameras	40
	Suspensions	41
	Transport for Civil Enforcement Officers	41
	The penalty charge	41
	Differential penalty charges	42
	The Penalty Charge Notice (PCN)	43
	Ensuring each PCN has a unique number	43
	Standard contraventions and associated code numbers	44
	Other points about the Penalty Charge Notice	44
	Collecting evidence of the contravention	45
	Service of the PCN at the time of the contravention	45
	Observation periods	47
	Loading and unloading	48
	Double parking and parking at dropped footways etc	49
	Double parking	49
	Parking alongside dropped footways etc	49
	Service of a PCN by post	50
	Prevention of service by force, threats of force, obstruction or violence	51
	Prevention of service by 'drive away'	53
	Return of the motorist before the CEO has started to issue the PCN	55
	Enforcement by approved devices	55
	Immobilisation/removal	58
	Special consideration for disabled badge holders and vehicles with diplomatic registration plates	61
	Persistent evaders	61
9	**Exemptions, waivers and dispensations**	63
	Blue Badge (disabled persons parking) Scheme	63
	Abuse of the Blue Badge scheme	65
	Targeted surveillance operations	65
	Working with the police	65
	Day-to-day enforcement inspections	65
	Power to inspect	66
	Withdrawing badges due to repeated misuse	68
	Reciprocal arrangements for disabled drivers from other countries	68
	Diplomatic registered vehicles	68
	Immobilisation	69

	Removal	69
	Recovery of unpaid PCNs	70
	Application to HM forces and visiting forces	71
	Waivers	71
	Dispensations for professional care workers	71
	Exemptions where parking places are suspended	72
	Miscellaneous exemptions	73
10	**Policy and administrative functions**	**74**
	Providing a quality service	74
	Collecting penalty charges	74
	Location of payment centres and opening hours	78
	Temporary waiving of payments	78
	Payments for release of a vehicle from an immobilisation device or a vehicle pound	79
	Issuing the Notice to Owner	79
	Information from DVLA about the registered keeper	81
	DVLA record is incomplete	82
	Diplomatic vehicles	83
	Charge Certificate	83
	Registering the Charge Certificate with the Traffic Enforcement Centre	84
	Witness Statement (formerly a Statutory Declaration)	84
	Warrants of Execution and Certificated Bailiffs	85
11	**Challenges, representations and appeals**	**89**
	Challenges – also known as informal representations	90
	Formal representations	92
	Representations against immobilisation or removal	95
	Consideration of representations	96
	Providing false information	97
	Notification of the outcome of representations	97
	Adjudication	98
	Cases referred back to the authority by the adjudicator	99
12	**Key criteria when applying for the power to enforce parking regulations**	**100**
	Other powers received along with the power to enforce parking	100
	Immobilisation and removal	100
	Bus lanes	101
	Special Enforcement Areas (SEAs)	101
	Authorities eligible to apply for CPE power	101
	Co-operation between district councils and county councils	102
	Consulting other local authorities	102
	Consulting other bodies	103
	The continuing role of the police	103

13 What an authority should do before taking on parking enforcement power — 105

Formulating and appraising parking policies — 105

Traffic Regulation Orders (TROs) — 105

Pavement parking — 107

Choosing the most appropriate package of enforcement measures — 107
- Enforcement on trunk roads and other high speed roads — 107
- Level of enforcement — 108
- Exemptions, waivers and dispensations — 108
- Assessment of the chosen enforcement package — 108

14 Financial assessment — 110

Parking charges — 112

Penalty charges — 113
- Discounts and increases to penalty charges — 114
- Estimating income from penalty charges — 115

Charges and income from vehicle immobilisation, removal, storage and disposal — 115

Publication of the level of penalty and other charges — 116

Changes to penalty and other charges — 117

VAT and penalty charge income — 117

15 Application for a CEA designation order — 118

Annexes

A What the civil enforcement of parking under the Traffic Management Act 2004 involves and how it differs from decriminalised parking enforcement under the Road Traffic Act 1991 — 130

B Enforcement action started under the Road Traffic Act 1991 — 136

C Contraventions for which the higher and the lower level penalty charges should be made — 137

D Examples of information that it may be prudent for a CEO to note — 140

E Appraising the adequacy of traffic signs, plating and road markings — 142

F Appraising Traffic Regulation Orders (TROs) and Traffic Management Orders (TMOs) — 144

G SIA guidance on vehicle immobilisation on private land — 154

H Abbreviations used in this publication — 157

Index — 158

CHAPTER 1
Introduction

1.1 Part 6 of the Traffic Management Act 2004 (TMA) provides for the civil enforcement of most types of parking contraventions. It replaces Part II and Schedule 3 of the Road Traffic Act 1991 and some local legislation covering London only.

1.2 This Operational Guidance:

- sets out the policy framework within which the Government believes that all English local authorities, both inside and outside London, should be setting their parking policies and, if appropriate, enforcing those policies;

- tells all English local authorities of the changes to parking policy and enforcement that result from the replacement of part II of the Road Traffic Act 1991 (RTA) by the parking provisions in part 6 of the Traffic Management Act 2004;

- advises all English enforcement authorities of the procedures that they **must** follow, the procedures to which they ***must have regard*** and the procedures that the Government recommends they follow when enforcing parking restrictions;

- tells those English local authorities who have not yet done so of the scope for taking over parking regulation enforcement from the police, and how to go about it; and

- tells members of the public, as well as local authorities, about parking policies and their enforcement.

1.3 This Operational Guidance is good practice guidance. It is not the guidance issued under section 87 of the Traffic Management Act 2004, although it quotes from that guidance – see paragraph 1.4 below. **Where it says that something must be done, this means that it is a requirement in either primary or secondary legislation, and a footnote gives the appropriate provision.** Where a statute imposes a duty on a local authority, a failure to comply will constitute a breach of statutory duty. This document **has no special authority in regard to matters of legal interpretation. Where there appear to be differences between the regulations and the Guidance, the regulations always take precedence.**

1.4 Wording in this document in **bold and Comic Sans MS typeface** is part of the Secretary of State for Transport's Guidance (often referred to as the Statutory Guidance) which **is published under section 87 of the Traffic**

Management Act 2004. section 87 of the TMA stipulates that local authorities *must have regard* to the information contained in that Guidance, which is available as a separate document.[1]

1.5 This Guidance replaces the joint Department for Transport and Welsh Office Circular 1/95 *Guidance on Decriminalised Parking Enforcement outside London* and relevant sections of the Mayor of London's Transport Strategy. You should read it in conjunction with the Road Traffic Regulation Act 1984 (RTRA), Part 6 of the Traffic Management Act 2004, and SIs 2007/3482,[2] 2007/3483,[3] 2007/3484,[4] 2007/3485,[5] 2007/3486[6] and 2007/3487.[7]

1.6 You should also read it alongside any guidance and Codes of Practice subsequently issued by the Government (available on the DfT website), by the Parking Adjudicators, London Councils[8] and the Local Government Association.

1.7 You should also take account of good practice guidance from organisations such as the:

- British Parking Association;
- Institution of Highways and Transportation;
- CSS (formerly the County Surveyors' Society);
- Local Government Technical Advisory Group (TAG); and
- London Technical Advisors Group (LoTAG).

1.8 You should also learn from other authorities and the police.

DfT
March 2008

---

1 http://www.dft.gov.uk/pgr/roads/tpm/tmaportal/tmafeatures/tmapart6/betterprkstatutoryguid.pdf

2 The Civil Enforcement of Parking Contraventions (England) Representations and Appeals Regulations 2007 (SI 2007/3482)

3 The Civil Enforcement of Parking Contraventions (England) General Regulations 2007 (SI 2007/3483)

4 The Removal and Disposal of Vehicles (Amendment) (England) Regulations 2007 (SI 2007/3484)

5 The Civil Enforcement Officers (Wearing of Uniforms) (England) Regulations 2007 (SI 2007/3485)

6 The Civil Enforcement of Parking Contraventions (Approved Devices) (England) Order 2007 (SI 2007/3486)

7 The Civil Enforcement of Parking Contraventions (Guidelines on Levels of Charges) (England) Order (SI 2007/3487)

8 Formerly the Association of London Government

CHAPTER 2
The policy context

National policy

2.1 *The Future of Transport* White Paper, published in July 2004, set out a long-term strategy for a modern, efficient and sustainable transport system backed up by sustained high levels of investment over 15 years. Effective management of the road network is a key part of this. The Traffic Management Act 2004 imposes an explicit duty on local authorities to manage their network so as to reduce congestion and disruption and to appoint a traffic manager. The Act also provides additional powers to do with parking, including increased scope to take over the enforcement of driving and parking offences from the police.

2.2 Parking policies need to be integral to a local authority's transport strategy. The second edition of the Department's *Full Guidance on Local Transport Plans*, published in December 2004, says that local authorities should have policies aimed at tackling congestion and changing travel behaviour. These could include restricting and/or charging for car parking.

2.3 Discussions about parking tend to concentrate on enforcement. But all local authorities need to develop a parking strategy covering on- and off-street parking that is linked to local objectives and circumstances. They then need Traffic Regulation Orders (TROs) to put it in place and appropriate traffic signs and road markings to show the public what the restrictions mean. This strategy needs to take account of planning policies and transport powers and consider the appropriate number of total spaces, the balance between short and long term spaces and the level of charges.

2.4 Local authorities have long been responsible for managing all on-street and some off-street parking, whether directly or indirectly. The relevant powers are in the Road Traffic Regulation Act 1984 (RTRA). The Road Traffic Act 1991 significantly changed the way that on-street parking restrictions are enforced. Before 1991, the police and traffic wardens were responsible for enforcement and income from fixed penalty notices (FPNs) went to the Exchequer. The police service found itself increasingly unable to resource parking enforcement and a number of forces supported the idea of another agency taking on the responsibility.

2.5 The road safety and congestion implications of this lack of enforcement were unacceptable, so the 1991 Act made it mandatory for London boroughs and optional for other local authorities to take on the civil enforcement of non-endorsable parking contraventions. When a local authority takes over this power from the police, staff employed directly or indirectly by them issue Penalty Charge Notices (PCNs) and the local authority keeps the income.

2.6 The legal framework for enforcement authorities[9] in England comprises Part 6 of the Traffic Management Act 2004 and the regulations to bring Part 6 into effect. The TMA and the associated regulations have given to English authorities outside London many powers already available to authorities in London, giving greater consistency across the country while allowing for parking policies to suit local circumstances. The framework aims to make the system fair as well as effective.

2.7 **This Guidance uses the same terminology as the TMA, so it refers to:**

- *Civil Parking Enforcement* **(CPE) rather than** *Decriminalised Parking Enforcement;*
- *Civil Enforcement Officer* **(CEO) rather than** *Parking Attendant;* **and**
- *Civil Enforcement Area* **(CEA) rather than** *Special Parking Area/ Permitted Parking Area* **(SPA/PPA).**[10]

2.8 There are some changes to parking contraventions. These mainly affect local authorities outside London. They are set out in Annex A. The procedures for enforcement action started under the RTA are set out in Annex B.

2.9 **CPE is a legal process. Enforcement authorities should make sure that their employees and contractors who operate CPE regimes have a clear and full understanding of what the law requires. If enforcement authorities are themselves uncertain about any aspects of these requirements, they should get the appropriate legal advice.**

Local policy

2.10 Each local authority should have a clear idea of what its parking policy is and what it intends to achieve by it. This applies whether or not an authority is responsible for enforcement. They should appraise their policy and its objectives regularly. When setting and appraising the policy, an authority should take account of the:

- existing and projected levels of parking demand;
- availability and pricing of on- and off-street parking;
- justification for and accuracy of existing Traffic Regulation Orders; and
- accuracy and quality of traffic signs and road markings that restrict or permit parking.

---

9 Traffic Management Act 2004, Schedule 8

10 Areas which immediately before 31 March 2008 are designated as Special Parking Areas in London or as Permitted Parking and Special Parking Areas outside London automatically become Civil Enforcement Areas on that date. See Traffic Management Act 2004 Schedule 8, paragraphs 2(4) and 8(4).

2.11 Enforcement authorities should also set and regularly appraise the:

- level of compliance with parking controls that they want to achieve;
- level of enforcement necessary to get such compliance;
- penalty charge bands; and
- resourcing and training of parking staff.

2.12 Whether or not they have CPE powers, authorities should make sure that their parking policies are not only appropriate in terms of place and time, but are properly underpinned by valid, up-to-date Traffic Regulation Orders. The restrictions need to be made clear to motorists through appropriate and legal traffic signs and road markings. A parking contravention is nearly always a breach of a provision of the TRO, which must have been made under the correct section of the RTRA. A flawed or inadequately signed order may be unenforceable and can significantly damage both the aims of enforcement and the public perception of its management.

2.13 Authorities should consult the public on their parking policies as they formulate or appraise them. They should seek the views of people and businesses with a range of different parking needs as well as taking into account the views of the police. Once they have finalised their parking policies, they should make them available to the public. Explaining the context and the purpose of parking policies can increase public understanding and acceptance. It can even help public acceptance of enforcement. Where possible, neighbouring authorities should work together to ensure a consistent approach to parking policy and its enforcement.

Parking provision

2.14 The Government's policy on parking provision is set out in Planning Policy Guidance Note (PPG) 13 *Transport*. Specific policy on parking provision for housing development is in Planning Policy Statement (PPS) 3 *Housing*.

2.15 The key thrust of the policy in PPG13 is that local authorities should use parking policies alongside other planning and transport measures to promote sustainable transport choices and reduce reliance on the car. To support this objective, PPG13 says that local authorities should not normally require developers to provide more spaces than the developer would want to. Authorities should also encourage shared parking, particularly in town centres. Where appropriate, they should control on-street parking near major developments that have limited on-site parking but which generate lots of journeys. This will help to minimise the displacement of parked vehicles to the streets surrounding the developments.

2.16 PPG13 says that local authorities should set maximum levels of parking provision. Annex D of PPG13 currently sets out national maxima for a range of developments above certain thresholds. The Government is reconsidering the policy on car parking provision for commercial development.

2.17 PPS3 advises local planning authorities to develop parking policies for their plan area with local stakeholders and local communities having regard to expected car ownership for planned housing in different locations, the efficient use of land and the importance of promoting good design.

2.18 A good practice report by the Institution of Highways and Transportation, supported by the Department for Transport, advises local authorities on developing parking strategies. This includes advice on how much parking to provide.[11]

---

11 Parking Strategies and Management – IHT – August 2005

CHAPTER 3
Objectives of civil enforcement

Policy objectives

3.1 CPE should contribute to the authority's transport objectives. A good CPE regime is one that uses quality-based standards that the public understands, and which are enforced fairly, accurately and expeditiously.

3.2 Enforcement authorities should aim to increase compliance with parking restrictions through clear, well designed, legal and enforced parking controls. CPE provides a means by which an authority can effectively deliver wider transport strategies and objectives. Enforcement authorities should not view CPE in isolation or as a way of raising revenue.

3.3 Enforcement authorities should design their parking policies with particular regard to:

- **managing the traffic network to ensure expeditious movement of traffic, (including pedestrians and cyclists), as required under the TMA Network Management Duty;**[12]
- **improving road safety;**
- **improving the local environment;**
- **improving the quality and accessibility of public transport;**
- **meeting the needs of disabled people**, some of whom will be unable to use public transport systems and depend entirely on the use of a car; and
- **managing and reconciling the competing demands for kerb space** of:
    - residents;
    - shops;
    - businesses;
    - visitors, especially where there are many tourist attractions and hotels;
    - pedestrians;
    - delivery vehicles;
    - buses, taxis, private hire vehicles and coaches;
    - cars;
    - bicycles; and
    - motorcycles.

---

12 See the Traffic Management Act 2004, section 16.

3.4 Authorities should appraise their parking policies, CPE regimes and associated regulatory framework (including penalty charge levels) when reviewing their Local Transport Plans (LTP). In London these are known as Local Implementation Plans (LIP). Authorities that do not have an LTP or LIP should appraise their parking policies when reviewing their local development framework or community strategy. They should take account of the information they collect as part of the parking enforcement process. It is also worth interviewing CEOs, who are in a unique position to identify changes to parking patterns, as well as office staff who see the challenges and representations and the reasons behind them.

3.5 Chapter 4 gives advice on appraisal.

CPE financial objectives

3.6 CPE is a means of achieving transport policy objectives. **For good governance, enforcement authorities need to forecast revenue** and expenditure **in advance. But raising revenue should not be an objective of CPE, nor should authorities set targets for revenue or the number of Penalty Charge Notices (PCNs) they issue.**

3.7 The judgement in *R v LB Camden (ex parte Cran)* made clear that the Road Traffic Regulation Act 1984 is not a revenue raising Act.

3.8 **Enforcement authorities should run their CPE operations (both on- and off-street[13]) efficiently, effectively and economically. The purpose of penalty charges is to dissuade motorists from breaking parking restrictions. The objective of CPE should be for 100 per cent compliance, with no penalty charges. Parking charges and penalty charges should be proportionate, so authorities should not set them at unreasonable levels. Any penalty charge payments received (whether for on-street or off-street enforcement) must only be used in accordance with section 55 (as amended) of the Road Traffic Regulation Act 1984.**

3.9 Previous guidance said that local authority parking enforcement should be self-financing as soon as practicable. This is still a sensible aim, but compliant applications for CPE (see Chapters 12 to 15) will be granted without the scheme being self-financing. However, authorities will need to bear in mind that if their scheme is not self-financing, then they need to be certain that they can afford to pay for it from within existing funding. The Secretary of State will not expect either national or local taxpayers to meet any deficit. Any application to the Secretary of State for a scheme that is not self-financing should be supported by a resolution of the full Council.

---

13 CPE can only apply to privately owned car parks that are regulated by an order made under the Road Traffic Regulation Act 1984, section 35 and provided under any letting or arrangements made by a local authority with some other person (such as a privately-owned company) under section 33(4) of that Act.

Applying for CPE powers in conjunction with neighbouring authorities may be one way of tackling a potential financial shortfall. But a robust agreement on cost sharing will be needed if the partnership is to last.

CHAPTER 4
Appraising, ensuring the effectiveness of and reporting on civil parking enforcement

Appraising CPE

4.1 Enforcement authorities should monitor their parking policies, CPE regimes and associated regulatory framework (including penalty charge levels). They should appraise them when reviewing their Local Transport Plans (LTP) (known as Local Implementation Plans – LIPs – in London) and make recommendations for improvements to members. If an authority does not have an LTP/LIP, the appraisal should be part of the review of the local development framework or community strategy.

4.2 Appraisals should take account of any relevant information that has been collected as part of the parking enforcement process, in particular about the practical effectiveness of the scheme. They will benefit from interviews with CEOs, who are in a unique position to identify changes to parking patterns, and with office staff, who see challenges and representations and the reasons for them.

4.3 The Secretary of State recommends that enforcement authorities consult locally on their parking policies when they appraise them. They should seek the views of people and businesses with a range of different parking needs as well as taking into account the views of the police.

4.4 The appraisal should take account of:

- existing and predicted levels of demand for parking;
- the availability and pricing of on- and off-street parking places;
- the justification for, and accuracy of, existing traffic orders;
- the adequacy, accuracy and quality of traffic signing and road markings which restrict or permit parking within or outside a Controlled Parking Zone;
- the level of enforcement necessary for compliance;
- the levels of penalty charges;

- the need to resource the operation effectively and ensure that all parking staff are appropriately trained; and
- impact on traffic flow, i.e. traffic or congestion outcomes.

4.5 The appraisal should ensure that parking policies still apply at the right place and time. It is particularly important to check that the policies are properly underpinned by TROs that are valid, up-to-date and properly indicated with traffic signs and road markings. A parking contravention is often a breach of a provision of a TRO, which must have been made under the correct section of the Road Traffic Regulation Act 1984 (RTRA).[14] **Flawed orders,** or inadequately or incorrectly signed orders, **may be unenforceable, and can damage both the aims of CPE and the public perception of how it is managed.**

4.6 As part of this appraisal, authorities should make sure that detailed operational policies remain appropriate. They should also tell the public about any changes to them.

4.7 As well as the day-to-day management of the in-house staff or contractors responsible for enforcing civil parking, local authority officers are responsible for reviewing the effectiveness of their authority's parking policies as a whole.

Ensuring the effectiveness of CPE

4.8 **Enforcement authorities can improve the efficiency and effectiveness of their CPE regimes by maintaining a regular dialogue – and undertaking joint activity where appropriate – with their on-street contractor (if there is one), the police, neighbouring authorities,** the Driver and Vehicle Licensing Agency (**DVLA**), **the Traffic Enforcement Centre (TEC) and representatives of road user groups.**

4.9 **In particular, authorities should maintain good relations with the police. The police continue to have responsibility for enforcing endorsable and most types of moving traffic offences, and for taking action against vehicles where security or other traffic policing issues are involved. Regular liaison will help to ensure that civil and criminal enforcement operate effectively. Good relations between the police and an enforcement authority can also help in tackling threats and abuse aimed at CEOs.**

4.10 **It is recommended that enforcement authorities keep abreast of developments in neighbouring authorities' CPE operations and look into the benefits of consistent, and possibly collaborative, approaches to enforcement.**

---

14 For complete lists of parking contraventions which are civilly enforceable, see the Traffic Management Act 2004, Schedule 7, Paragraphs 2, 3 and 4.

4.11   Authorities should develop good working relations with the DVLA, in particular with regards local authorities receiving keeper information promptly. Authorities should also consider helping the DVLA track down Vehicle Excise Duty (VED) evaders by notifying them of any vehicles that are not displaying a valid VED disc.

4.12   As far as possible, the performance of contractors and of staff should be judged according to how far desired transport objectives have been achieved. An enforcement authority should base performance measures and rewards or penalties, wherever possible, on outcomes rather than outputs. Performance and rewards/penalties should never be based on the number of PCNs, immobilisations or removals. Outcome indicators might include compliance statistics, the number of appeals, the number and length of contraventions and the localised impact they appear to have had on road safety and congestion. Incentives could work towards good customer service. For example, indicators for immobilisation and removals might be based on the release time of the vehicle after the owner has paid the appropriate fees.

4.13   When enforcement operations are carried out 'in house', there should be a service level agreement (SLA) incorporating the specification terms and conditions required by the client department – the same as for a contract with an external service provider.

4.14   The Secretary of State recommends that enforcement authorities use a balanced SLA or model contract, such as the one developed by the British Parking Association.[15]

Reporting

4.15   Reporting is an important part of accountability. The transparency given by regular and consistent reporting should help the public understand and accept CPE. Monitoring also provides the authority with management information for performance evaluation and helps to identify where it needs to improve its CPE regime. It provides a framework for performance comparisons between councils. Reports should include the benefits that any net parking income has helped to pay for.

4.16   Enforcement authorities should produce an annual report about their enforcement activities within six months of the end of each financial year. The report should be published and as a minimum it should cover the financial, statistical and other data (including any parking or CPE targets) set out below.

---

15   For further details contact the BPA ref: Parking Model Contract 2005 or go to http://www.britishparking.co.uk

4.17 Enforcement authorities should make annual returns to the Government about the number and speed of payment of PCNs. They should also advise the appropriate adjudication service in a timely fashion how many PCNs they have issued.

4.18 Authorities may want to include information that allows their performance to be assessed over time and measured against that of comparable authorities. The Secretary of State recommends that each authority should publish the report on their website and place copies in civic offices and local libraries.

4.19 There are likely to be benefits to authorities from collecting and comparing management information on other aspects of civil parking enforcement operations. These could include the grounds on which representations and appeals are made, the number of CEOs employed, and the average number of appeals per officer.

4.20 Authorities should also publish a code of practice that their CEOs must follow. This will need to be handled with care. It may help to pre-empt criticism if the authority makes the following points:

- the authority is committed to delivering good quality public services;
- the code of practice is to ensure that high quality parking enforcement is delivered fairly and in accordance with the law;
- parking restrictions are there for good reasons – to improve safety, prevent congestion, ensure a fair distribution of parking spaces, and help reduce pollution; and
- parking restrictions should be enforced efficiently, fairly and with proper regard to the rights of the motorist.

4.21 Authorities should measure their parking enforcement performance to show that it is just for traffic management purposes. They might include management information such as:

- cutting the number of vehicles that contravene restrictions and how long they contravene them for;
- reducing public transport journey times across the CEA;
- reducing the number and severity of road traffic casualties in the area of enforcement;
- reducing congestion in the area of enforcement;
- frequency of CEO patrols, especially where contraventions are high;
- percentage of PCNs appealed against;
- percentage of successful appeals; and
- percentage of vehicles immobilised that are released within a specified time of the declamping fee being paid; and

- percentage of representations and other correspondence answered within a specified time. This target should be the same as, or more stretching than, other targets that the authority has set for responding to correspondence.

4.22 Authorities could include performance against these targets in their annual report or publicise it on their website. They might also publicise it periodically in the local press. They should certainly make it available to anyone who requests it. When comparable information is available, authorities should track their performance against similar authorities. If this assessment is not favourable, they should consider how they might improve.

4.23 Any contract to provide parking enforcement should have sufficient incentives to achieve the targets set out in the code of practice. However, these should not involve targets for the number of PCNs issued, or vehicles immobilised or removed. Contractors should be rewarded for their contribution to transport objectives – safety and network management in particular.

4.24 Key stakeholders, as well as the Secretary of State, would be pleased to receive a copy of an authority's annual report.

Parking Annual Reports: possible contents

Financial

- Total income and expenditure on the parking account kept under section 55 of the Road Traffic Regulation Act 1984 as modified by regulation 25 of the Civil Enforcement of Parking Contraventions (England) General Regulations 2007 (see paragraphs 4.27 to 4.29 below);
- Breakdown of income by source (i.e. on-street parking charges and penalty charges);
- Total surplus or deficit on the parking account;
- Action taken with respect to a surplus or deficit on the parking account;
- Details of how any financial surplus has been or is to be spent, including the benefits that can be expected as a result of such expenditure.

Statistical

- Number of higher level PCNs issued;
- Number of lower level PCNs issued;
- Number of PCNs paid;
- Number of PCNs paid at discount rate;
- Number of PCNs against which an informal or formal representation was made;
- Number of PCNs cancelled as a result of an informal or a formal representation;

- Number of PCNs written off for other reasons (e.g. CEO error or driver untraceable);
- Number of vehicles immobilised;
- Number of vehicles removed.

Performance against targets
- Performance against any parking or CPE targets. Authorities should note the recommendations throughout this Guidance on the areas where such targets might be appropriate.

Financial reporting

4.25 The income and expenditure of local authorities in connection with their on-street charging and their on-street and off-street enforcement activities are governed by section 55 (as amended) of the Road Traffic Regulation Act 1984. This means that *all* their income and expenditure *as enforcement authorities* (i.e. related to the issue of and income from PCNs) in respect of off-street parking places is covered by section 55. London authorities must[16] keep an account of all income and expenditure in respect of designated (i.e. on-street) parking places; and their functions (income and expenditure) as enforcement authorities, within paragraphs 2 and 3 of Schedule 7 to the TMA. English authorities outside London must[17] keep an account of all income and expenditure in respect of designated (i.e. on-street) parking places which are not in a Civil Enforcement Area, income and expenditure in designated (i.e. on-street) parking spaces which are in a Civil Enforcement Area and their functions (income and expenditure) as an enforcement authority.

4.26 The Secretary of State has included a provision in the TMA that further amends section 55 RTRA. This provision affects any local authority that enforces civil parking. It means that their on-street parking account is no longer limited to permitted parking income and expenditure. The on-street parking account will also include income and expenditure for all restricted parking contraventions within a CEA – on-street as well as off-street. Local authorities should be able to distinguish between income from off-street and on-street penalty charges, but will need to find a way of allocating costs between the two. The report should cover all on-street income from and expenditure on parking activities, including parking meters, pay-and-display machines, residents' parking permits and penalty charge notices. **All enforcement authorities in London must**[18] **send a copy of the account to the Mayor of London** as soon as reasonably possible after the end of the financial year.

---

16 See amendments to section 55 Road Traffic Regulation Act 1984 in S.I. 2007/3483, regulation 25

17 S.I. 2007/3483, regulation 25

18 S.I. 2007/3483, regulation 25

4.27 **Where an authority makes a surplus on its on-street parking charges and on- street and off-street enforcement activities, it must[19] use the surplus in accordance with the legislative restrictions in section 55 (as amended) of the RTRA 1984.**

4.28 The Secretary of State recommends that enforcement authorities publish this account in their annual report.

4.29 Every local authority makes financial returns each year to Communities and Local Government. These returns include information about parking income and expenditure.

Returns to Government on enforcement action

4.30 Each year, enforcement authorities should tell the Government how many:

- higher level PCNs they issued for parking contraventions;
- lower level PCNs they issued for parking contraventions;
- PCNs were paid;
- PCNs were paid at the discount rate (14 or 21 days as appropriate);
- representations (formal and informal) were made against PCNs;
- PCNs they cancelled as a result of an informal or a formal representation;
- PCNs they wrote off for other reasons (for example, CEO error or motorist untraceable);
- vehicles they immobilised; and
- vehicles they removed.

4.31 The figures should cover PCNs issued and vehicles immobilised or removed in 2007 and subsequent calendar years. The other data should also cover the period for which the returns are requested, even though the action may not relate to the PCN, immobilisation or removal activity in that period.

---

19 S.I. 2007/3483, regulation 25.

CHAPTER 5
Consultation and communication with the public

5.1 Parking policies and their enforcement are complex. They can confuse the public if they are not explained clearly. People often do not understand why we need parking restrictions or how they help to keep traffic moving and roads safe. Consultation and communication are the foundation of a fair and effective parking policy. They help to ensure that the public understands and respects the need for enforcement. Consultation should be an ongoing process that takes place whenever an authority proposes major changes and at regular intervals after that.

Consultation

5.2 The Secretary of State expects local authorities considering major changes to their parking policies to consult fully with stakeholders. As a minimum, local authorities should consult the following groups:

- those involved in the implementation and operation of parking, including the police, neighbouring local authorities, the DVLA and the Traffic Enforcement Centre;
- wider stakeholders with an interest in parking, including businesses, motoring groups and representative organisations; and
- those who will be affected, including residents, motorists and the general public. Authorities should include socially excluded groups.

5.3 Authorities should consider setting up their own user group for wider stakeholders such as businesses, representative organisations and the public. This should comprise representatives of motoring organisations, local residents and traders, socially excluded groups and others with an interest in parking policies. This group can be used to test proposals to ensure they meet the needs of road users.

5.4 Loading and unloading can be a recurrent and difficult problem. Authorities should work with deliverers, local businesses and residents to tackle problems at hotspots. They should establish dialogue with deliverers (for example through Freight Quality Partnerships) and regularly review the delivery environment. Authorities should have particular regard for the security and health and safety issues surrounding the handling of high value or bulky consignments. They should consider how they can best meet the needs of those who handle such consignments without endangering or inconveniencing other road users.

5.5 Local authorities will need to publicise their consultation document and make it available in hard copy and on the web. They need to set a deadline for feedback – central government consultations usually allow 12 weeks. In any broad consultation like this, local authorities will need to show that they have made every effort to gain representative feedback from stakeholders.

5.6 After the consultation has closed, authorities should provide a public response which outlines the feedback they received and what they have done to take this feedback on board.

Communication

5.7 **It is important that the public understand why an authority has introduced CPE and what parking restrictions are in place. Motorists and other road users need to be aware that parking enforcement is about supporting wider transport objectives, in particular** road safety and **keeping traffic moving, rather than raising revenue.**

5.8 **It is also important that motorists and other road users understand the details of the scheme,** including the areas covered by CPZs and enforcement times. **Unclear restrictions, or restrictions that do not comply with regulations or with the Secretary of State's Guidance, will confuse people and ultimately undermine the operation and enforcement of the scheme overall. Once authorities have finalised their parking enforcement policies, they should publish and promote them openly.** Communications can never substitute for clear traffic signs and road markings. But informing the public of what an authority is trying to achieve through CPE should increase both understanding and compliance. Advance warning is particularly important where a local authority proposes introducing immobilisation or vehicle removal operations.

5.9 **Enforcement authorities should consider the full range of media available to them when communicating with the public. They should consider telling every household in the CEA when they propose changes e.g. to the operation of a scheme.**

5.10 Authorities are likely to get a relatively large number of queries or complaints when CPE is first introduced and need a comprehensive communication plan. The Cabinet Office[20] gives guidelines on communication with the public. This covers:

- media campaigns on plans for CPE;
- email/direct mail to key stakeholders;

---

20   www.cabinetoffice.gov.uk/regulation/consultation

- briefing events;
- public speaking opportunities;
- one-to-one meetings with key organisations; and
- public events and engagement opportunities for staff.

5.11 Authorities need to let people know at least four weeks before introducing CPE, and explain what it will mean in practice and the benefits of the system. Local authorities may choose to use the following sorts of activity.

Leaflets and posters – these are effective as they can reach people where they make decisions about parking – on the street, in car parks, or even when they have just received a PCN. They can also be distributed through shops, local councils, parishes and libraries.

Website – useful for communicating complex information about parking enforcement. Material on websites will still need to be available in other formats so that partially sighted people and those without internet access are not disadvantaged.

Local press and broadcast media – a good way to communicate to a broad cross-section of the community.

Public forums and other local events – a good opportunity to speak to people face-to-face and to keep them informed about local parking issues.

Paid-for advertising – should complement communications activity as part of an integrated, long-term programme.

Electronic updates – developing an e-community of interested stakeholders makes it easy to keep people informed about parking enforcement. A regular newsletter coupled with e-updates has worked well for some local authorities.

Direct communications – such as phone and e-mail to answer queries correctly and promptly.

5.12 **There should be regular communication after CPE is introduced and when changes are made.**

5.13 **Enforcement authorities should try to work regularly with neighbouring authorities to ensure a consistent approach to communication, across regions and not just local boundaries, as well as to enforcement.**

Content of parking communications

5.14 Authorities should cover the following subjects:

- changes to parking enforcement including what people will experience and how the system will differ (where relevant);
- the benefits of CPE and what it will mean for people;

- where motorists can park, both on-street and off;
- exemptions, waivers and dispensations;
- when vehicles might be immobilised or removed;
- PCNs and how to avoid getting one – do not assume that people know what a PCN is or that they know all the parking rules;
- a succinct summary of the representations and appeals process;
- how to pay a PCN, including contact numbers; and
- where to get more information.

5.15 Communicate with the public in plain English. Follow the Plain English Campaign's Crystal Mark guidelines.[21]

---

21 www.plainenglish.co.uk

CHAPTER 6
Training and professionalism in civil parking enforcement

6.1   Once a solid foundation of policies, legitimate TROs, and clear and lawful signs and lines are in place, the success of CPE will depend on the dedication and quality of the staff that deliver it. It is essential to give staff at all levels the skills and training to do their jobs effectively if the service is to command public confidence and respect. This should also improve the self-esteem and job satisfaction of staff, resulting in higher retention rates. Training should be seen as a legitimate and important aspect of CPE running costs and training budgets should be protected from cuts.

6.2   The office processes involved in CPE are important and staff carrying them out need similar levels of skill, training and professionalism as the more visible on-street enforcement officers. Enforcement authorities should provide enough staff for the volume of work. They should also make sure that those staff (whether employed directly by the authority or by a contractor to deal with informal challenges) have the skills, training, authority and resources to give the public a high-quality, professional, efficient, timely and user-friendly service.

6.3   **Authorities that outsource any area of parking enforcement to private companies should ensure that the contractor fulfils all the requirements set down for the authority itself.** The British Parking Association – with the help of the Department for Transport – has produced a model contract for employing civil enforcement contractors. The Secretary of State recommends that local authorities use this or a similar document if they contract out their parking enforcement. If their own staff carry out enforcement, they should use the same sort of performance and management provisions as those set out in the model contract.

6.4   Authorities should make sure that all Civil Enforcement Officers (CEOs), back office staff, supervisors and managers are trained to provide accurate, fair and consistent enforcement. The training needs to take place before they start work and at regular intervals – perhaps every other year – during their career. This requirement applies whether the authority employs CEOs directly or through a contractor. It is the authority's responsibility to ensure that an appropriate training programme is in place.

Back office and management staff

6.5 Authorities can sometimes overlook the importance of good-quality, well-trained back office and management staff. They are just as important for a fair and effective CPE regime. All civil enforcement staff should be trained in general enforcement procedures and any special requirements of the authority. Most, but not all, aspects of general (or 'core') training will be relevant to all authorities. For instance, some authorities may not use parking vouchers or meters.

6.6 In addition, supervisory and managerial staff will need training in:

- Government transport policy and objectives;
- the role of parking regulations and enforcement;
- the legal framework for civil parking enforcement;
- applying the authority's published policies;
- parking contravention codes and descriptions, and their use;
- challenges and representations; and
- mitigation.

Civil Enforcement Officers (CEOs)

6.7 **CEOs are the public face of CPE and the way they perform their functions is crucial to the success, and public perception, of an authority's CPE operation.** Authorities and their service providers should carefully consider the skills and attributes that CEOs need. They should set out assessment criteria that will allow them to recruit or contract suitable personnel.

6.8 CEOs need to be professional and efficient, sometimes in difficult circumstances. The public needs to see them this way too. CEOs need firmness, sensitivity and tact coupled with common sense and patience. And they need to think clearly and react sensibly under pressure. CEOs who lack these qualities should get appropriate training and development opportunities.

6.9 Under the TMA 2004, enforcement authorities are responsible for considering any representations against PCNs. Consistently high enforcement standards should keep the number of representations down. Authorities should make it clear to CEOs that their job is to enforce the controls fairly with a view to achieving high levels of compliance. In practice this means that authorities need to ensure that all CEOs, whether employed or contracted, are:

- competent and willing;
- supervised effectively; and
- properly trained and clearly instructed about their conduct.

6.10 **CEOs may be required to work near schools and similar sensitive areas and be seen as a uniformed figure of authority. The Secretary of State recommends that an applicant for a job as a CEO undergoes a Criminal Records Bureau check.** There should also be regular checks of CEOs once employed. The enforcement authority can check criminal records itself, as can another organisation that employs CEOs, or an umbrella organisation, as long as they meet the conditions of registration. These are that the organisation is entitled to ask exempted questions under the Rehabilitation of Offenders Act 1974 Exceptions Order 1975, and is a registered body or uses the services of a registered umbrella body. Further information is on the CRB website.[22]

CEO duties

6.11 **The main objective of a CEO should be to ensure parking controls are observed and enforced in a fair, accurate and consistent manner.** CEOs must comply with the national legislation that applies to all local authority staff, even if they are employed through a contractor.

6.12 The main duties of a CEO on patrol are:

- enforcing parking regulations by serving PCNs where vehicles are parked in contravention of the restrictions. They may complete a PCN by hand or using a hand-held computer (HHC). A PCN must be fixed to the vehicle or given to whoever appears to be in charge of it. Besides the information which must be recorded on the PCN, it is important that CEOs use their HHC or a separate pocket book to note any other relevant information. This may be needed when considering representations and appeals. Increasingly, CEOs also record evidence using a digital camera (See Chapter 8); and

- logging all their daily activity in their HHC or pocket book. The log should record any evidence additional to that on the PCN or entered into the HHC or their pocket book when a PCN is issued and non-enforcement activities, such as conversations with members of the public or other CEOs, noting missing lines or signs, or defective meters or pay-and-display machines.

6.13 **CEO duties will also include related activities such as the following:**

- Helping the public and acting as the first point of contact on minor parking enquiries and enforcement matters;

- **Inspecting parking equipment.** Checking that parking meters and pay-and-display machines are working before issuing a PCN. CEOs may be able to fix minor faults, but if not they should put an 'out of order' notice on the meter or machine and report the fault. In the case of pay-and-display machines, CEOs should only issue a PCN if there is an alternative machine in working order nearby that covers the same parking place;

---

[22] www.crb.gov.uk

- **Checking and reporting defective traffic signs and road markings.** This includes signs that are obscured, damaged, or deliberately 'spun round', and broken or faded road markings. Defective or missing signs or lines may make the Traffic Regulation Order (TRO) that they indicate unenforceable, in which case CEOs should not issue a PCN;

- **Issuing information leaflets or warning notices;**

- **Providing witness statements** for the line manager when reporting that they were unable to serve a PCN because they were obstructed, threatened with violence or the vehicle was driven away;

- **Providing witness statements** for a parking adjudicator when deciding on a written appeal from a motorist. These should only be needed in exceptional circumstances;

- **Where appropriate, appearing before a parking adjudicator.** This is not expected to be a normal or frequent part of the duties of an effective CEO. Authorities need to consider whether a CEO who regularly issues PCNs that are appealed against needs to improve his or her performance;

- Recommending priority cases for immobilisation or removal of vehicles, in accordance with priority ranking and local policies. However, another civil enforcement officer who has received extra training should actually authorise the immobilisation or removal (see Chapter 8); and

- Reporting suspected Blue Badge abuse.

6.14 The TMA encourages authorities to take a comprehensive approach to traffic management and use parking policies and their enforcement as part of this rather than an isolated activity. Any parking attendant appointed under section 63A of the Road Traffic Regulation Act 1984 by an enforcement authority becomes a CEO in relation to parking contraventions. They may be appointed a CEO in relation to other road traffic contraventions for which they are the enforcement authority[23]. The TMA does not repeal section 63A. section 63A provides that parking attendants (now CEOs) shall also have such other functions in relation to stationary vehicles as may be conferred by or under any other enactment. The Secretary of State's view is that CEOs should only be used for duties related to those road traffic contraventions that their authority is responsible for enforcing. **If CEOs have time, the authority may wish to consider asking them to carry out tasks such as the following:**

- **informing the police of criminal parking activity;**

- **reporting suspected abandoned vehicles;**

- **reporting vehicles with no valid tax disc to the DVLA;**

- **putting in place and removing notices about the suspension of parking places;**

- **checking that shops selling parking vouchers have adequate stocks;**

---

23   TMA, section 76(5)

- reporting on changes in parking patterns;
- assisting with on-street enforcement surveys; and
- checking that non-mobile objects in parking places (for example, skips) are in compliance with the authority's licence.

6.15 It is important that these supplementary duties do not stop CEOs carrying out their principal duties and that the authority complies with the restrictions on the use of parking income set out in section 55 (as amended) of the RTRA.[24]

Discretion

6.16 The Secretary of State considers that the exercise of discretion should, in the main, rest with back office staff as part of considering challenges against PCNs and representations against a Notice to Owner – NtOs. This is to protect CEOs from allegations of inconsistency, favouritism or suspicion of bribery. It also gives greater consistency in the enforcement of traffic regulations.

6.17 However, the enforcement authority may wish to set out certain situations when a CEO should not issue a PCN. For example, an enforcement authority may wish to consider issuing a verbal warning rather than a PCN to a driver who has committed a minor contravention and is still with, or returns to, the vehicle *before* a PCN has been served. The enforcement authority should have clear policies, instructions and training for CEOs on how to exercise such authority. These policies should form the basis for staff training and should be published.

Training

6.18 Authorities should recognise the importance of their role in ensuring that their contractor recruits suitable personnel and gives them the appropriate training, equipment, guidance and supervision.

6.19 Enforcement authorities should ensure that CEOs are properly trained to enforce parking controls fairly, accurately and consistently. As well as formal training, it is recommended that authorities include some supervised on-street training to familiarise CEOs with the area and any special parking provisions. Enforcement authorities should make sure that CEOs understand all relevant exemptions, such as those applying to diplomatic vehicles and the Blue Badges issued to disabled people. CEOs should be aware of their powers

---

24 IS.I.2007/ 3483, regulations 25 and 26

to inspect Blue Badges[25] **and the sensitivity required should they need to exercise them. It is recommended that all CEOs achieve minimum standards through recognised training courses.**

6.20 There are formal qualifications for CEOs. The national qualifications for CEOs are the S/NVQ in parking control and the City and Guilds Level 2 Certificate for Civil Enforcement Officers (Parking).[26] It is recommended that CEOs hold the level 2 nationally accredited qualification. This is listed on the national qualification framework (or future equivalents) and cross-referenced to the national occupational standard in parking control.

6.21 Authorities should ensure that training equips CEOs with the interpersonal, conflict resolution and oral communication skills they need to perform their jobs effectively and without undue stress or personal danger. They should have regular refresher training. Training may be based on existing qualifications or similar ones, but authorities should always supplement these with further training relevant to local needs and policies.

6.22 General training for CEOs should cover issues that all the staff and contractors of the authority need to know, plus:

- introduction to the role and duties of CEOs;
- understanding the legal foundation and objectives of CPE;
- how the system works in practice;
- types of permitted and restricted parking;
- the role of the police and the parking offences that remain their sole responsibility;
- types of civil parking contraventions;
- the PCN, including the information it must contain, standard contravention codes and optional suffixes and additional details for use by the authority if a penalty charge is disputed;
- the difference between higher and lower level PCN contraventions;
- waivers, exemptions and dispensations;
- exemptions for vehicles displaying a Blue Badge, how the Blue Badge scheme works, the reciprocal arrangements for disabled drivers from outside the United Kingdom, and an awareness of the problems faced by disabled people;
- provisions on loading and unloading;
- provisions on picking up and setting down;
- the vehicle registration system, including foreign and diplomatic registrations;

---

25 Department for Transport: Guidance on the inspection and enforcement of Blue Badges for police, traffic wardens, local authority parking attendants, civil enforcement officers and issuing local authorities.

26 Details at www.city-and-guilds.co.uk

- use of pocket books, including use of standard characters and how to deal with erasures, lost pages, crossings out, etc;

- use of hand-held computers, including daily test routines, recording data accurately and rectifying common faults;

- use of PCN printing equipment, whether integrated with the HHC or a separate unit, including changing paper and batteries and minor maintenance on a shift;

- use of digital cameras, whether integrated with the HHC or separate units, and how to take digital pictures that are relevant and good enough to be used as supporting evidence;

- use of communication devices and the phonetic alphabet;

- requirements concerning uniforms;

- PCNs not served because of violence, threat of violence, obstruction or drive-aways;

- use of verbal warnings;

- patrol methods, including both general principles and specific advice on enforcing different types of parking control (such as loading only restrictions, permitted parking at parking meters);

- dealing with the general public, including conflict management and aggressive motorists;

- emergency procedures, including CEO responsibilities, use of communication devices, and personal security;

- the need to operate within the law and, in particular, not to break traffic regulations whilst enforcing them;

- the adjudication service, including the preparation of witness statements; and

- on-street practice of techniques.

6.23 CEOs will also need training in the procedures drawn up by their employing authority, including:

- discretionary exemptions, waivers and dispensations (see Chapter 9);

- other special exemptions, for example any period of grace between permitted parking time elapsing and issue of a PCN;

- observation periods;

- 'mitigating circumstances' and other matters which require CEOs to use their judgement;

- liaising with other parts of the enforcement operation, such as immobilisation or removal teams, or the PCN processing unit;

- liaising with the police and traffic wardens to deal with illegally parked vehicles;

- complaints by members of the public; and

- other aspects of enforcement specific to the authority, such as type of HHC used, standards expected of CEOs, and type of voucher, parking meter and pay-and-display machine used.

6.24 CEOs will need further training if they work for an authority that operates a vehicle immobilisation or removal service, as will the vehicle immobilisation and removal staff themselves (see below). This should deal with the criteria and procedures that a CEO should apply when recommending vehicles for immobilisation or removal. Senior enforcement officers or other selected CEOs who will authorise immobilisation or removals will need extra training. You can find advice on the procedures for recommending and authorising immobilisation or removal in Chapter 8.

6.25 Organisations representing disabled people, freight hauliers and motorists may be happy to contribute to sections of a course in which they have a special interest.

Probation

6.26 Following training, CEOs should serve a probationary period of at least four weeks, during which they should be closely supervised. CEOs should not patrol unaccompanied until they have been assessed as competent to do so to the authority's satisfaction.

Camera operators

6.27 Where enforcement is based on CCTV surveillance, authorities should make sure that operators have specialised training. Current guidance is for operators to achieve the BTEC qualification. You can find further advice in the *Code of Practice for Operation of CCTV Enforcement Cameras*[27] and *A code of practice for bus lane camera enforcement using attended CCTV equipment for approved English Local Authorities Outside London.*[28]

Immobilisation and removal teams

6.28 Members of immobilisation and/or removal teams should be fully trained in legal requirements, public relations and the need to advise vehicle owners of their right to make representations and appeals.

6.29 The Home Office set up the Security Industry Association (SIA) under the Private Security Industry Act 2001. The SIA regulates the private security industry in England and Wales. It licenses vehicle immobilisers who carry out their activities on private land against a release fee. If an

---

27 Available at www.londoncouncils.gov.uk
28 Available at http://www.manchester.gov.uk/site/scripts/download_info.php?fileID=4429

authority uses a firm that also works on private land, they should make sure that all of the company's operatives hold licences. You can find the SIA guidance for vehicle immobilisers on private land at annex G.

6.30 Vehicle owners may be unsure whether the firm that has immobilised or removed their vehicle is working on private or local authority-owned land, or on the public highway. The confusion is likely to be greatest on private roads. Enforcement authorities may wish to require their immobilisation or removal teams to wear uniforms that clearly identify the authority on whose behalf they are working and which also carry a personal identification number. Authorities may consider using liveried vans and (if used) immobilisation devices to avoid confusion with operators on private land.

CHAPTER 7
Choice and certification of devices for camera enforcement

7.1   Devices used to enforce parking contraventions **must**[29] be certified by the Secretary of State. Devices used for enforcement in London before 31 March 2008 may be used for a transitional period of 12 months until 30 March 2009. After that, they too must either be certified by the Secretary of State or replaced. The Vehicle Certification Agency[30] (VCA) certifies devices on behalf of the Secretary of State.

Devices certified by the Secretary of State

7.2   All devices used to enforce parking restrictions have to meet the requirements of paragraphs 2 to 6 of the Schedule of SI 2007/3486. These apply to fully automatic systems and those that need a CCTV operator.

7.3   A device may be designed and produced by one manufacturer. Alternatively, it may be specified by a system designer and incorporate sub-systems and/or equipment produced by one or more manufacturer.

7.4   You can find detailed information about how the legal requirements will be assessed, and how to apply for certification in *Civil Traffic Enforcement – Certification of Approved Devices*.[31] This includes guidance on the choice and operation of suitable equipment. You can get further advice about the procedure from:

Vehicle Certification Agency
1 The Eastgate Office Centre
Eastgate Road
Bristol
BS5 6XX

01179 515151
www.vca.gov.uk

---

29 S.I. 2007/3486

30 VCA is an executive agency of the Department for Transport. It is the United Kingdom's national approval authority for new road vehicles, agricultural tractors and off-road vehicles.

31 http://www.dft.gov.uk/pgr/roads/tpm/tmaportal/tmafeatures/tmapart6/certapproveddevices.pdf

Procedures for operating parking enforcement systems

7.5 Each enforcement authority must have procedures in place to preserve the integrity of evidence from CCTV cameras and handle and store it securely. The procedures should satisfy the community over the competence and honesty of the system and its operators. They should also reassure the community over the privacy of private areas and domestic buildings and comply with the requirements of the Data Protection Act 1998.

7.6 The organisation London Councils has produced a code of practice covering the operation of CCTV cameras, to ensure consistency of enforcement across London. Elements of this code could act as a guide to authorities outside London. You can get copies of this code of practice from London Councils.[32]

7.7 You can get advice on the requirements of the Data Protection Act 1998 and any subsequent amendments from the Information Commissioner's website.[33]

7.8 The CCTV User Group[34] also provides members with general advice and model documents on the use of all types of CCTV systems. These model documents include *CCTV User Group Code of Practice* and *Model Procedures Manual*.

7.9 Authorities should develop procedures for operating all parking enforcement systems in consultation with the manufacturer(s).

---

[32] www.londoncouncils.gov.uk
[33] www.informationcommissioner.gov.uk
[34] www.cctvusergroup.com

CHAPTER 8
Enforcement

8.1 The public and the press are likely to judge parking enforcement by how it is carried out on the streets and in car parks. It is, therefore, important that authorities enable CEOs to do their job properly by giving them the right training (Chapter 6) and up-to-date equipment.

Civil Enforcement Officers' handbook

8.2 The local authority should produce a handbook for CEOs. This should be based on the training given to CEOs and could be used both as part of that training and as a guide to procedures for officers on duty. The handbook should explain the different types of parking contravention. Many authorities that already have civil parking enforcement powers, and service providers, have handbooks which can be used as a model.

8.3 An authority could prepare a handbook alongside the specification for tenderers wishing to provide CEO services. Alternatively, an authority could require the contractor to provide a suitable handbook. The authority should check that the instructions in any handbook produced by a contractor comply with the law and this Guidance.

Uniforms

8.4 **When exercising prescribed functions**[35] **a CEO must**[36] **wear a uniform. The uniform should** be readily distinguishable from those worn by the police and traffic wardens, and **clearly show:**

- **that the wearer is engaged in parking enforcement;**
- **the name of the local authority/authorities of whose behalf s/he is acting; and**
- **a personal identity number.**

8.5 The 'specified' functions to which the requirement to wear a uniform applies are the issuing of PCNs on the street and authorising or carrying out the immobilisation or removal of vehicles within a CEA. Where someone acting under the direction of a CEO actually immobilises or removes the vehicle, that person is not obliged to wear a uniform in compliance with this Guidance.

---

35 TMA, section 78(2)(a) and (b) and section 79, and Road Traffic Regulation Act 1984, section 99
36 TMA, section 76(3)(a)

However, if an authority carries out immobilisations or removals, it may wish to ensure that the operatives wear uniforms that show clearly a personal identity number and the enforcement authority.[37] This should help prevent confusion with operatives working on private land, for the police or for DVLA.

8.6 If appropriate headgear, such as a hat, is part of the uniform, the civil enforcement officer should wear it at all reasonable times, unless unable to do so for religious reasons. It may be sensible to make headgear optional in certain circumstances so that a PCN is valid even if issued by a CEO not wearing a hat.

8.7 **It is recommended that CEOs carry a photo-identity card, showing their identification number and the name of their employer. However, to protect the safety of staff, it is strongly recommended that the photo-identity card does not include the CEO's name on it.**

8.8 Staff working in CCTV control rooms do not have to wear uniforms, but an authority may prefer them to.

Equipment

Hand-held computers

8.9 The Secretary of State recommends that CEOs use a hand-held computer (HCC) to issue PCNs. However, to ensure business continuity, they should still be able to write them by hand if necessary. The advantages of HHCs over handwritten PCNs are:

- they can transfer information quickly and cheaply to other computers for further processing or storage;
- PCNs do not have to be cancelled because of illegible handwriting;
- they can be programmed to correct common mistakes such as inputting the wrong contravention code, street name or officer identification number;
- additional information such as details of a conversation with a driver can be typed into the HHC, making it easily available when considering representations and appeals;
- details of vehicles used by persistent evaders or non-payers, or vehicles with invalid permits, can be downloaded from a central database to HHCs at the start of each shift;
- some HHCs can list repeat contraveners or non-payers who frequently park in particular streets;
- information about the number and location of different parking contraventions and the performance of different CEOs can be collected quickly and cheaply. Analysis of this information should help make on-street enforcement more efficient; and

---

37 S.I. 2007/3485

- some HHCs transmit information directly between CEOs and their base, eliminating the need for a separate radio.

8.10 Authorities should choose an HHC that can transmit and receive data readily to and from other systems used elsewhere in the enforcement process – including, where necessary, systems used by other enforcement authorities.

8.11 The CEO or a manager should check the internal clock in HCCs at least daily to ensure accuracy. They should synchronise them with the clocks on pay-and-display machines.

8.12 If a CEO needs to test an HHC before preparing a PCN, they should be careful which vehicle registration number they input. The test could access a live record held by DVLA, and a PCN could accidentally be issued to an innocent motorist. Personal data from DVLA records must be used for fair and lawful purposes and its use for anything other than an actual parking contravention could break data protection rules. They should not use ABC 123, as this is an actual registration number. Authorities should test HHCs using the registration number of a vehicle whose owner works in the parking department and who knows what to do if the test PCN is not deleted.

8.13 HHCs vary significantly in price and performance, depending on the quality and sophistication of the software. An authority planning to buy or lease HHCs needs to consider the purchase or hire costs, plus maintenance and the cost of consumables such as ribbons and paper rolls. The most important consideration is that the HHC should have enough memory to include the authority's street index and any databases used for enforcement purposes. It is also important to check that the batteries will last for the length of an entire beat or patrol.

Mobile communications

8.14 An authority or contractor will have greater control over the movement of CEOs if they are issued with mobile phones or radios. This means that, for example, complaints from the public can be dealt with quickly. CEOs will also be able to contact senior staff for advice, or request help (for example, if they are being threatened). A mobile phone will allow CEOs to tell the police about criminal parking offences, or request a police presence. Direct communication between CEOs and the despatch controller is highly desirable – if not essential – where a vehicle is to be immobilised or removed (see below).

Digital cameras

8.15 Photographs from digital cameras help reduce the potential for disputes about facts. They reduce the likelihood of an appeal and if an appeal is held, they improve the speed and quality of justice. They are particularly useful in cases where, for example, a vehicle is not parked correctly within a bay or one or more of its wheels contravenes a parking order. They can also be useful to rebut claims that a PCN was not attached to a vehicle. However, digital photographs are not *necessary* to prove that a contravention took place.

8.16 Given the greater cost and inconvenience of removal, the Secretary of State recommends that all vehicles are photographed before they are moved, so that any later dispute about their position or condition can be resolved. Authorities operating vehicle removals should consider issuing digital cameras to CEOs authorising removals, or to removal operatives.

8.17 Digital images need to be good quality, clearly display the nature of the contravention and the surrounding environment and show the date and time stamps.

Suspensions

8.18 Civil enforcement officers on enforcement duty sometimes have to suspend parking bays, meters and the like. They need a minimum amount of standard equipment to do this. All cones, tape, bags for meters or pay-and-display signs, and 'cover over' signs for bay signs should clearly identify the enforcement authority and, if appropriate, the contractor.

Transport for Civil Enforcement Officers

8.19 CEOs may spend some of their time walking to and from their beats. Local traffic conditions will determine whether this lost time can be reduced by providing them with transport.

The penalty charge

8.20 The penalty charge is usually payable by the owner of the vehicle, except if the vehicle was hired at the time of the contravention. The legislation gives the owner the right to make a representation against the Notice to Owner. They also have the right to appeal to an independent adjudicator if dissatisfied with the authority's decision to reject a representation. If an owner has not made a representation or appeal, or they have made one but it was rejected, and they have still not paid the PCN, the authority may issue a Charge Certificate. This means that the penalty charge is recoverable through the Traffic Enforcement Centre as a civil debt due to the authority. This is enforceable through a streamlined version of the normal civil debt recovery process. See also Chapters 10 and 11.

8.21 Although London enforcement authorities set the levels of penalty charges applicable in Greater London, the Mayor of London has to approve them. The Secretary of State has reserve power to object if s/he considers that some or all of the charge levels are excessive. The Mayor also determines how the levels of charges should be published by Transport for London and the London local authorities.

8.22 Each enforcement authority outside London **must**[38] set its own level of penalty charges. The level of those charges **must**[39] follow the guidelines set out in the Schedule to the Guidelines on Levels of Charges Order.[40] When authorities outside London change the levels of their penalty charges they **must**[41] publish these new charges in at least one local newspaper 14 days or more before the new charges come into effect.

Differential penalty charges

8.23 The Secretary of State and the Mayor of London have agreed that authorities must set two levels of penalty charges with the higher level applying to the more serious contraventions. Differential penalty charges were introduced in London in July 2007 and outside London on 31 March 2008. **Parking in a place where it is always prohibited (such as on a red route, on double yellow lines, or in a disabled bay without displaying a valid badge) is considered more serious than overstaying where parking is permitted (e.g. in a parking place). There is a perceived unfairness of receiving the same penalty regardless of the seriousness of the contravention. For this reason, and in order to emphasise the traffic management purposes of CPE, enforcement authorities must**[42] **apply different parking penalties to different contraventions. Outside Greater London, the current three-band system has been reduced to two, and the higher and lower penalty charges in these bands are specified in the Guidelines Order.**[43] **The full lists of contravention codes is set out by the London Councils and reproduced in** Annex C. **The higher list is specified in the Guidelines Order.**[44] **This Order will be varied from time to time and enforcement authorities should check with the London Councils and on the DfT website that they are using the most up-to-date version.**

Table 8.1: PCN levels outside London from 31 March 2008

Band	Higher level penalty charge	Lower level penalty charge
1	£60	£40
2	£70	£50

---

38 TMA, Schedule 9, paragraph 7
39 TMA, Paragraph 8
40 S.I. 2007/3484
41 TMA, Schedule 9, Paragraph 9
42 S.I. 2007/3487.
43 S.I. 2007/3487, Schedule
44 S.I. 2007/3487, Annex of the Schedule

Table 8.2: PCN levels in London from July 2007

Band	Higher level penalty charge	Lower level penalty charge
A	£120	£80
B	£100	£60
C	£80	£40

8.24 The Secretary of State will review the bands of penalty and other charges from time to time and will consult interested parties. Authorities outside London will be told when the Secretary of State changes the bands and levels outside London. Up-to-date figures will be published on the DfT website. When new penalty charge levels are introduced, authorities need to advise the public at least 14 days before they come into force.

8.25 A joint committee of all the local authorities reviews the levels of penalty charges in London. Transport for London reviews the levels of charges on roads for which the Greater London Authority (GLA) is responsible. Any proposed changes are subject to the approval of the Mayor of London and may not be introduced if the Secretary of State has objected. You can find up-to-date figures on the levels of penalty charges in London on the London Councils website in the 'Parking Enforcement Explained' section.

The Penalty Charge Notice (PCN)

Ensuring each PCN has a unique number

8.26 All Penalty Charge Notice (PCN) numbers should be unique and must have 10 characters.

8.27 The first two characters of each number should be unique to a particular authority. An authority seeking CPE power should contact the manager of the Traffic Enforcement Centre (TEC), Northampton County Court at an early stage to request a prefix that has not already been allocated (see Chapter 10 for the Centre's address and a description of its role).

8.28 The next seven digits uniquely identify the PCN within the authority's area. This means that each authority can have up to 9,999,999 numbers before having to start again.

8.29 The final character of each PCN number will be a check digit. This is designed to validate the PCN number (for example, by detecting typing errors when numbers are being processed). The Traffic Enforcement Centre can advise on the formula to use for calculating the check digit. No PCN number should ever be reused without the prior consent of the Traffic Enforcement Centre.

Standard contraventions and associated code numbers

8.30 There is a single, nationwide list of contraventions and associated code numbers and suffixes. This enables statistics on the operation of the powers in different authority areas to be collected consistently. It also makes the system easier for motorists who commit contraventions in more than one area to understand, and should help authorities using common systems to co-operate. A parking adjudicator dealing with cases from two or more authorities will find it easier to interpret the standard contravention descriptions and codes.

8.31 The standard contravention codes are numbers (01, 02, and so on). Gaps have been left at the end of each category so that further contraventions can be added. Authorities can add optional suffixes (b, d, p, etc.) to clarify the contravention, depending, for example, on the types of parking bays it uses. The Traffic Enforcement Centre des not see optional suffixes.

8.32 The driver should be able to read the PCN and understand why it was issued. The code on its own is not enough.

8.33 The contravention codes are now divided into two lists. One sets out the codes of contraventions to which the higher level penalty charge applies and the other sets out the contraventions to which the lower level penalty charge applies.

8.34 The Secretary of State expects all applications for designation orders to confirm that the enforcement authority will use the standard contravention code list issued by the London Councils. This is revised from time to time and available on their website. All authorities operating CPE will be told of any changes or additions, as long as they have given London Councils their contact details.[45] Authorities need to make sure that they keep London Councils up-to-date with their contact details. Authorities should exclude from their list any codes that are not relevant to their area (for example, because they have no free parking bays, or a particular contravention is not covered by any order in the authority's area). They should not change the code numbers.

Other points about the Penalty Charge Notice

8.35 Authorities should not issue PCNs when traffic signs or road markings are incorrect, missing or not in accordance with the TRO. These circumstances may make the Order unenforceable. If a representation against a PCN shows that a traffic sign or road marking was defective, the authority should accept the representation because the adjudicator is likely to uphold any appeal. An enforcement authority may be acting unlawfully and may damage its reputation if it continues to issue PCNs that it knows to be unenforceable.

---

45 parking@londoncouncils.gov.uk

Collecting evidence of the contravention

8.36 The local authority must[46] provide evidence of the contravention either from a CEO's direct observation, or from the record of an approved device.[47]

Service of the PCN at the time of the contravention

8.37 **The PCN must[48] either be fixed to the vehicle or given to the person who appears to be in charge of that vehicle, although there are three exceptions to this**[49] (see paragraph 8.63 below). The CEO should be clearly visible at all times when issuing a PCN. If an authority serves a PCN by post because the CEO was threatened or the vehicle owner drove away (see below), they will need to ensure that their standard procedures enable them to refute allegations that the CEO was not clearly visible.

8.38 The vehicle owner's copy of the PCN should be fixed to the windscreen, so it must be weatherproof or able to fit a weatherproof envelope. It should be fixed in such a way that it cannot easily be removed by wind or passers-by.

8.39 Hand-held computers can transfer details of PCNs electronically to a central database. This system should prevent any changes to the data once the PCN is issued. A second printed copy can be produced automatically at any time, so the CEO does not need to produce one when serving the PCN. Details recorded this way are admissible in proceedings before an adjudicator, but need to be a copy of the original in the sense of reproducing all of the text exactly. If the PCN is written by hand, the CEO needs to produce two copies. One is served and the other kept by the authority for monitoring payment and dealing with representations, including any which go before an adjudicator.

8.40 **A PCN** served on the vehicle or to the person who appears to be in charge of the vehicle (a 'regulation 9' PCN) **must contain**[50] **the** following **information:**

- the date on which the notice is served;
- the name of the enforcement authority;
- the registration mark of the vehicle involved in the alleged contravention (that is, the number plate);
- the date and time at which the alleged contravention occurred;
- the grounds on which the CEO serving the notice believes that a penalty charge is payable;

---

46   S.I. 2007/3483, regulation 6
47   A device specified in S.I. 2007/3486
48   S.I. 2007/3483, regulation 9
49   S.I. 2007/3483.regulation 10(1)
50   S.I. 2007/3483, Schedule, Paragraphs 1, and S.I. 2007/3482 , regulation 3(2)

- the amount of the penalty charge;
- The manner in which the penalty charge must be paid;
- that the penalty charge must be paid not later than the last day of the period of 28 days beginning with the date on which the PCN was served;
- that if the penalty charge is paid not later than the last day of the period of 14 days beginning with the date on which the notice is served, the penalty charge will be reduced by the amount of any applicable discount – currently 50 per cent;
- that if the penalty charge is not paid before the end of the period of 28 days beginning with the date on which the PCN was served, a notice to owner (NtO) may be served by the enforcement authority on the owner of the vehicle;
- that a person on whom an NtO is served will be entitled to make representations to the enforcement authority against the penalty charge and may appeal to an adjudicator if those representations are rejected;
- that, if representations against the penalty charge are received at such address as may be specified for the purposes before an NtO is served:
- those representations will be considered;
- but that, if an NtO is served not withstanding those representations, representations against the penalty charge must be in the form and manner and at the time specified in the NtO.

8.41 **It is recommended that the PCN also gives:**

- **vehicle make and colour (if evident);**
- **detailed location of vehicle (full street name);**
- **the contravention code;**
- **observation start and finish times** (where appropriate);
- **PCN number (all PCNs should be uniquely identifiable);**
- **CEO's identification number;**
- **the vehicle's tax disc number and expiry date** (give reason if not recorded);
- amount of penalty time (when relevant); and
- serial number and expiry time of pay-and-display ticket or voucher (when relevant).

8.42 Permitted parking places can be identified on the PCN by meter number, parking place or bay number or the name of the car park. Describing the location in terms of street name only is unlikely to be enough if there is permitted and prohibited parking along it. The location should be clearly and unambiguously described using the HHC.

8.43 **Photographs and notes by the CEO about the circumstances should be kept as further evidence that the contravention took place and to help resolve any disputes. Authorities should provide CEOs with the appropriate equipment, training and guidance to collect such evidence in the circumstances that the authority has prescribed. The use of**

digital cameras and similar technology is strongly encouraged. Authorities should disclose their evidence at the earliest possible opportunity.

8.44   The CEO should record any additional information on their copy of the PCN or on the HHC. This allows the authority to make validation checks, resolve disputes, evaluate representations and respond to appeals. Annex D sets out the sort of additional information that it may be prudent to note.

8.45   A vehicle may be parked in contravention of more than one restriction. For example, it may be parked partly on a yellow line and partly in a marked bay with an inadequate parking ticket. In these circumstances the CEO should issue only one PCN. CEOs should be instructed on which contravention takes precedence.

8.46   If two or more PCNs are issued within 24 hours for the same contravention, that is, to a vehicle that has not been moved, it is current practice to cancel the second PCN. It may be sensible to review both PCNs and cancel the one with the least robust evidence. For instance, if the digital photograph for one was taken in the daytime and the other at night, the one taken in the light may well be clearer. If one PCN is at the higher rate and the other at the lower rate, the lower rate PCN should normally be considered first for cancellation.

8.47   It is important to put relevant information on the PCN's payment slip so that payment is assigned to the correct case. This should include the PCN number and the vehicle registration mark, plus other identifiers such as the date and time of issue, or a barcode that contains that same information. It is recommended that the payment slip states the amount of the penalty charge, so that even if it becomes detached from the notice, the recipient knows how much is due.

Observation periods

8.48   CEOs need to observe a vehicle for a time to ascertain whether certain contraventions are taking place. How long depends on the type of contravention. Authorities need to set these observation periods and make sure that their CEOs follow them. In the interests of open government, authorities may wish to publish the observation periods. Neighbouring authorities covering a continuous urban area should consider setting the same observation periods, as drivers may not know exactly where one local authority area ends and another starts.

8.49   There are two types of observation: casual and continuous. For casual observation, the standard procedure is for the CEO to note vehicle details when they first see a possible contravention taking place and to return a short while later or at intervals to see whether there is any sign of loading or unloading. If not, the CEO will issue a PCN.

8.50 For continuous observation, the standard procedure is for the CEO to note the vehicle details when they first see a possible contravention taking place and stay next to or near the vehicle, keeping it in sight at all times, for a set period (usually at least five minutes) to see if there is any sign of loading or unloading. If not, the CEO will issue a PCN.

8.51 A period of continuous observation, without any sign of the activity, provides better evidence that loading or unloading was not taking place. However it should not be considered conclusive proof, even after a relatively long observation period, as there are circumstances which could prevent the CEO from seeing the loading or unloading. Casual observation allows the CEO more freedom of movement and lets them cover a larger area, which may be more useful at busy times.

8.52 An observation period is not a grace period. A grace period is a period of time where a contravention is taking place but the authority chooses not to enforce.

Loading and unloading

8.53 Parking restrictions vary from area to area and so visitors may not be familiar with them. This is why it is important for traffic signs and road markings to indicate the restrictions clearly. Delivery drivers may be among those who are genuinely unfamiliar with the restrictions. They may also fail to comply with restrictions that they think do not take account of what they see as their legitimate need to load and unload. This does not justify committing a contravention, but authorities should include local businesses and representatives of logistics companies in their consultations and, as far as possible, consider their needs when developing parking and enforcement policies. They should also establish regular dialogue with deliverers (for example through Freight Quality Partnerships).

8.54 Authorities should ask applicants seeking planning permission for new commercial developments or, where appropriate, changes to or within commercial use, to provide adequate loading and unloading facilities. This should help cut the number of parking contraventions.

8.55 The rules for loading and unloading differ from those for other parking activities. Traffic orders that restrict or prohibit waiting in a street usually exempt the loading or unloading of goods. The precise nature of such an exemption will depend on the terms of the order. Some authorities designate on-street parking places just for loading. Where waiting for the purpose of loading is prohibited or restricted, the traffic signs and road markings must show the extent of the prohibition or restriction.

8.56 Loading or unloading must be continuous while the vehicle is parked in restricted areas. It is therefore important to clarify to CEOs that loading or unloading includes taking goods to where the recipient may reasonably be taken to require them in the premises, waiting for them to be checked, getting delivery or collection documents signed and returning to the vehicle. Delivery staff are expected to secure their vehicle when they are not with it and a vehicle can legitimately be locked during some of these stages. Once the delivery process is complete, however, the driver must move the vehicle even if it is within the maximum period allowed for loading or unloading.

Double parking and parking at dropped footways etc

8.57 **The TMA enables authorities with CPE power to enforce in a Special Enforcement Area (SEA)[51] prohibitions of double parking[52] and parking at dropped footways[53] as if they had been introduced using a Traffic Regulation Order (Traffic Management Order in London). Any Special Parking Area that existed before commencement of the TMA 2004 automatically becomes an SEA[54] but authorities should ensure that the public are aware of the new restrictions before starting enforcement.** In most authorities the area covered by their SPA was the same as their PPA, and so the area of the SPA will be the same as their CEA.

8.58 There are various exceptions to the prohibitions, set out in the TMA. Principally they cover:

- vehicles parked wholly within a designated parking place or any other part of the carriageway where parking is specifically authorised;
- vehicles used by the fire, ambulance or police services; and
- loading and unloading.

8.59 The provisions in the Act mean that an authority can introduce such a prohibition without a TRO/TMO, but that outside London traffic signs or road markings must show where the prohibitions apply. Many such prohibitions are already indicated – for instance, at street corners. Authorities can get guidance on appropriate indicators from the Signs Branch in DfT. Restrictions on the situations in which an authority can use these powers means that they may be more suitable for tackling persistent problems than occasional ones. An authority that decides to use the power should publicise when they will or will not do so before using it.

Double parking

8.60 The contravention of double parking applies when a vehicle parks on any part of the carriageway and no part of the vehicle is within 50 cm of the edge of the carriageway, subject to the exemptions in part 6 of the TMA.

Parking alongside dropped footways etc

8.61 The Highway Code advises drivers "DO NOT stop or park ... where the kerb has been lowered to help wheelchair users and powered mobility vehicles, in front of an entrance to a property or where you would obstruct cyclists' use

---

51 TMA, Schedule 10.
52 TMA, section 85.
53 TMA, section 86.
54 TMA, Schedule 10, paragraphs 1(5) and 3(5).

of cycle facilities ... except when forced to do so by stationary traffic." The contravention of parking adjacent to a dropped footway applies where a vehicle parks on the carriageway next to a place where the footway, cycle track or verge has been lowered to the level of the carriageway (or where the carriageway has been raised to the level of the footway, cycle track or verge) to assist:

- pedestrians crossing the carriageway;
- cyclists entering or leaving the carriageway; or
- vehicles entering or leaving the carriageway across the footway, cycle track or verge.

8.62 The contravention does not apply to specified exemptions, such as the emergency services, alighting, unloading, building works, road works, and the like. Nor does it apply where a vehicle is parked outside residential premises with the occupier's consent (but it does apply if that consent has been paid for). This exception does not apply in the case of a shared driveway. This exception suggests that authorities should not take enforcement action where a vehicle is parked outside residential premises unless the occupier has asked the enforcement authority to do so. Authorities will need to check that the individual making such a request is entitled to do so.

Service of a PCN by post

8.63 **There are three circumstances in which a PCN** (a 'regulation 10' PCN) **may be served by post:**[55]

- **where the contravention has been detected on the basis of evidence from an approved device;**
- **if the CEO has been prevented, for example by force, threats of force, obstruction or violence, from serving the PCN either by affixing it to the vehicle or by giving it to the person who appears to be in charge of that vehicle; and**
- **if the CEO had started to issue the PCN but did not have enough time to finish or serve it before the vehicle was driven away and would otherwise have to write off or cancel the PCN.**

8.64 **In any of these circumstances a PCN is served by post on the owner (whose identity is ascertained from the DVLA), and also acts as the Notice to Owner. The Secretary of State suggests that postal PCNs should be sent within 14 days of the contravention.**

---

55 S.I. 2007/3483, regulation 10.

Prevention of service by force, threats of force, obstruction or violence

8.65 A PCN may be served by post if someone intervenes to stop the CEO from serving it. This includes situations where the person who appears to be in charge of the vehicle is abusive, intimidatory or threatens or uses actual physical force. Authorities should contact the police about serious cases.

8.66 In these circumstances, the actual PCN issued by the CEO on patrol cannot be served by post because it does not give enough information. The authority should cancel the regulation 9 PCN prepared by the CEO and serve a regulation 10 PCN by post. Enforcement authorities should make sure that they have sufficient primary and supporting evidence to deal with any subsequent representations and appeals and any police action against the person who prevented service. They will also wish to obtain a witness statement from the CEO. Back-office staff should trace the registered keeper's address via the DVLA. In these circumstances the owner gets 14 days discount period for payment of the PCN. The PCN, which serves also as the NtO, **must** be served by first class post.[56] It **must** state:[57]

- the date of the notice, which must be the date on which it is posted;
- the name of the enforcement authority;
- the registration mark of the vehicle involved in the alleged contravention;
- the date and time at which the alleged contravention occurred;
- the amount of the penalty charge;
- the manner in which the penalty charge must be paid;
- the grounds on which the enforcement authority believes that a penalty charge is payable;
- that the penalty charge must be paid not later than the last day of the period of 28 days beginning with the date on which the PCN is served;.
- that if the penalty charge is paid not later than the last day of the period of 14 Days, beginning with the date on which the PCN was served, the penalty charge will be reduced by any applicable discount – currently 50 per cent;
- that if after the last day of the period of 28 days beginning with the date on which the penalty charge notice is served, no representations have been made in accordance with regulation 4 of the Representations and Appeals Regulations ('regulation 4'), and the penalty charge has not been paid, the enforcement authority may increase the penalty charge by the amount of any applicable surcharge – currently 50 per cent – and take steps to enforce payment of the charge as so increased;
- the amount of the increased penalty charge;

---

[56] S.I. 2007/3483, regulation 3 (1)
[57] S.I. 2007/3483, Schedule 1, paragraph 2 and S.I. 2007/3482, regulation 3(4)

- that the PCN is being served by post because a CEO attempted to serve a PCN by affixing it to the vehicle or giving it to the person in charge of the vehicle but was prevented from doing so by some person;

- that representations on the basis specified in regulation 4 may be made to the enforcement authority against the imposition of the penalty charge but that representations made outside the period of 28 days, beginning with the date on which the PCN is served may be disregarded;

- the nature of the representations which may be made under regulation 4;

- the address (including, if appropriate, any e-mail address or fax telephone number, as well as the postal address) to which representations must be sent;

- the form in which they (the representations) must be made;

- that if representations which have been made within the representation period or outside the period but not disregarded, are not accepted by the enforcement authority the recipient of the PCN may appeal against the authority's decision to an adjudicator.

8.67 **It is recommended that the PCN also gives:**

- **vehicle make and colour (if evident);**
- **detailed location of vehicle (full street name);**
- **the contravention code;**
- **observation start and finish times** (where appropriate);
- **PCN number (all PCNs should be uniquely identifiable);**
- **CEO's identification number; and**
- **the vehicle's tax disc number and expiry date** (give reason if not recorded);
- amount of penalty time (when relevant);
- serial number and expiry time of pay-and-display ticket or voucher (when relevant).

8.68 The regulations set out how an authority **must**[58] calculate the date of service of a postal PCN. Unless proved otherwise, service is taken to have been on the second working date after posting. A working day excludes a Saturday, a Sunday, New Year's Day, Good Friday, Christmas Day and any other English bank holiday. The date of posting is not necessarily the same as the date on which the back office staff prepare the PCN, and authorities should make sure that their procedures take account of this.

---

58 S.I. 2007/3483, regulation 3(2) and regulation 3(3)

Prevention of service by 'drive away'

8.69 A PCN may also be served by post if the CEO had begun to issue it – i.e. has completed his/her observations and had either started to write the PCN or put the data into the HHC and would, in other circumstances, have to cancel the PCN – but the vehicle was driven away before the CEO had time to finish or serve the PCN.

8.70 In such circumstances, the actual PCN issued by the CEO on patrol cannot be sent by post because it does not give enough information. The authority should cancel the regulation 9 PCN prepared by the CEO and serve a regulation 10 PCN by post. Enforcement authorities should make sure that they have sufficient primary and supporting evidence to deal with any subsequent representations and appeals. They will also wish to obtain a witness statement from the CEO. The Secretary of State recommends that the CEO records the vehicle's licence number and tells the driver of the contravention before they drive away. Back-office staff should obtain the registered keeper's home address from DVLA. In these circumstances the motorist gets a 14 day discount period. The PCN, which serves also as the NtO, **must** be served by first class post.[59] It must state:[60]

- the date of the notice, which must be the date on which it is posted;
- the name of the enforcement authority;
- the registration mark of the vehicle involved in the alleged contravention;
- the date and time at which the alleged contravention occurred;
- the amount of the penalty charge;
- The manner in which the penalty charge must be paid;
- the grounds on which the enforcement authority believes that a penalty charge is payable;
- that the penalty charge must be paid not later than the last day of the period of 28 days beginning with the date on which the PCN is served;.
- that if the penalty charge is paid not later than the last day of the period of 14 Days, beginning with the date on which the PCN was served, the penalty charge will be reduced by any applicable discount – currently 50 per cent;
- that if after the last day of the period of 28 days beginning with the date on which the penalty charge notice is served, no representations have been made in accordance with regulation 4 of the Representations and Appeals Regulations ('regulation 4'), and the penalty charge has not been paid, the enforcement authority may increase the penalty charge by the amount of any applicable surcharge – currently 50 per cent – and take steps to enforce payment of the charge as so increased;
- the amount of the increased penalty charge;

---

[59] S.I. 2007/3483, regulation 3(1),

[60] S.I. 2007/3483, Schedule 1, paragraph 2 and S.I. 2007/3482, regulation 3(4)

- that the PCN is being served by post because a CEO had begun to prepare a PCN for service in accordance with regulation 9 (by affixing it to the vehicle or giving it to the person in charge of the vehicle) but the vehicle was driven away from the place in which it was stationary before the CEO had finished preparing the PCN or had served it in accordance with regulation 9;

- that representations on the basis specified in regulation 4 may be made to the enforcement authority against the imposition of the penalty charge but that representations made outside the period of 28 days, beginning with the date on which the PCN is served may be disregarded;

- the nature of the representations which may be made under regulation 4;

- the address (including, if appropriate, any e-mail address or fax telephone number, as well as the postal address) to which representations must be sent;

- the form in which they (the representations) must be made;

- that if representations which have been made within the representation period or outside the period but not disregarded, are not accepted by the enforcement authority the recipient of the PCN may appeal against the authority's decision to an adjudicator.

8.71 **It is recommended that the PCN also gives:**

- **vehicle make and colour (if evident);**
- **detailed location of vehicle (full street name);**
- **the contravention code;**
- **observation start and finish times** (where appropriate);
- **PCN number (all PCNs should be uniquely identifiable);**
- **CEO's identification number;**
- **the vehicle's tax disc number and expiry date** (give reason if not recorded);
- amount of penalty time (when relevant); and
- serial number and expiry time of pay-and-display ticket or voucher (when relevant).

8.72 The regulations set out how an authority **must**[61] calculate the date of service of a postal PCN. Unless proved otherwise, service is taken to have been on the second working date after posting. A working day excludes a Saturday, a Sunday, New Year's Day, Good Friday, Christmas Day and any other English bank holiday. The date of posting is not necessarily the same as the date on which the back office staff prepare the PCN, and authorities should make sure that their procedures take account of this.

---

61 S.I. 2007/3483, regulation 3(2) and regulation 3(3)

8.73 Even if service is prevented, CEOs should try to collect information and photographic evidence as usual. Authorities should provide CEOs with the equipment, training and guidance to collect such evidence, bearing in mind that they may find this harder where service is being prevented. Authorities should disclose their evidence at the earliest possible opportunity.

8.74 If the keeper recorded on the DVLA database was not the keeper at the time of the contravention, the authority may issue a second postal PCN/NtO to the person who was the actual owner at the time.[62]

8.75 Authorities will wish to record which CEOs ask for regulation 10 PCNs to be issued. If they find that some officers experience more 'drive aways' than others, they may wish to consider whether there is anything in the way that these officers work that contributes to this.

Return of the motorist before the CEO has started to issue the PCN

8.76 CEOs should continue to issue a PCN once they have started. If this causes the vehicle owner difficulties, the CEO should show them the procedures set out on the PCN for lodging representations.

8.77 A PCN **may not**[63] be served by post if the motorist returns to the vehicle before the CEO has started to issue it. A CEO has not started to issue a PCN if s/he is observing a vehicle or jotting down some details. It is only when the CEO starts to create the PCN and would otherwise have to cancel it that they have started to issue it. If the driver returns before the CEO has started to issue the ticket, the CEO should establish whether the vehicle is parked in contravention (for example, if loading or unloading is taking place). If the vehicle is in contravention, the CEO should ask the driver to comply with the restrictions.

Enforcement by approved devices

8.78 **TMA regulations**[64] **give the power to authorities throughout England to issue PCNs for contraventions detected with a camera and associated recording equipment (approved device). The Secretary of State must**[65] **certify any type of device used solely to detect contraventions (i.e. with no supporting CEO evidence)** as described in Chapter 7. **Once certified they may be called an 'approved device'.** Motorists may regard enforcement by cameras as over-zealous and authorities should use them sparingly. The Secretary of State recommends that authorities put up signs to tell drivers that they are using cameras to detect contraventions. Signs must comply with TSRGD[66] or have special authorisation from DfT. **The Secretary of State recommends that**

---

62   S.I. 2007/3483, regulation 10(5) combined with S.I. 2007/3482, regulation 4(4)
63   S.I. 2007/3483, regulation 10(2)
64   S.I. 2007/3483, regulation 10
65   S.I. 2007/3486 and S.I. 2007/3483, regulation 10
66   Diagrams 878 and 879

approved devices are used only where enforcement is difficult or sensitive and CEO enforcement is not practical. Approved devices should not be used where permits or exemptions (such as resident permits or Blue Badges) not visible to the equipment may apply.

8.79 **The primary objective of any camera enforcement system is to ensure the safe and efficient operation of the road network by deterring motorists from breaking road traffic restrictions and detecting those that do. To do this, the system needs to be well publicised and indicated with lawful traffic signs.**

8.80 Authorities should make sure that they have procedures to stop the service of two PCNs – one at the time of the contravention and one by post with evidence from an approved device.

8.81 Authorities should design a system so that fully trained staff are able to:

- monitor traffic in accordance with a Code of Practice;
- identify the registration number, colour and type of a vehicle contravening traffic restrictions;
- support the serving of a PCN to the registered keeper of a vehicle contravening the restrictions;
- record evidence of each contravention to ensure that representations and appeals can be answered fully;
- produce timed and dated pictorial evidence of any unauthorised driving or stopping to be produced as information to the registered keeper and for any subsequent representations or appeals; and
- immediately despatch a CEO and removal truck for targeted enforcement of vehicles contravening traffic restrictions.

8.82 An essential and integral part of any system is a code of practice. This sets out the objectives of the system and the rules it will follow. Authorities should ensure that they produce (or adopt) and follow a code of practice. The code should make sure that staff deal properly with issues such as privacy, integrity and fairness. It should set minimum standards to help ensure public confidence in the scheme.

8.83 Authorities **must**[67] give a discount period – currently 21 days – for a PCN issued on the basis of evidence from an approved device. This is because the PCN also serves as the Notice to Owner, so the motorist does not have the opportunity to make representations against it. The 21 day discount period for PCNs sent by post using evidence from approved devices is longer than that for PCNs sent by post for bus lane contraventions and certain moving traffic contraventions (the latter power is only available in London at the moment). The Government intends to consult on bringing the two periods into line.

---

67 S.I. 2007/3483, Schedule 1, Paragraph 3

8.84 PCNs for contraventions detected by an approved device cannot be placed on the vehicle or handed to the person who appears to be in charge of the vehicle. They are sent by post to the keeper using data from DVLA. The PCN sent by post on the basis of evidence produced by an approved device serves also as a Notice to Owner. It **must**[68] state:

- the date of the notice, which must be the date on which it is posted;
- the name of the enforcement authority;
- the registration mark of the vehicle involved in the alleged contravention;
- the date and time at which the alleged contravention occurred;
- the amount of the penalty charge;
- The manner in which the penalty charge must be paid;
- the grounds on which the enforcement authority believes that a penalty charge is payable;
- that the penalty charge must be paid not later than the last day of the period of 28 days beginning with the date on which the PCN is served;
- that if the penalty charge is paid not later than the last day of the period of 21 Days, beginning with the date on which the PCN was served, the penalty charge will be reduced by any applicable discount – currently 50 per cent;
- that if after the last day of the period of 28 days beginning with the date on which the penalty charge notice is served, no representations have been made in accordance with regulation 4 of the Representations and Appeals Regulations ('regulation 4'), and the penalty charge has not been paid, the enforcement authority may increase the penalty charge by the amount of any applicable surcharge – currently 50 per cent – and take steps to enforce payment of the charge as so increased;
- the amount of the increased penalty charge;
- that the PCN is being served by post on the basis of a record produced by an approved device;
- that representations on the basis specified in regulation 4 may be made to the enforcement authority against the imposition of the penalty charge but that representations made outside the period of 28 days, beginning with the date on which the PCN is served may be disregarded;
- the nature of the representations which may be made under regulation 4;
- the address (including, if appropriate, any e-mail address or fax telephone number, as well as the postal address) to which representations must be sent;
- the form in which they (the representations) must be made;
- that if representations which have been made within the representation period or outside the period but not disregarded, are not accepted by the enforcement authority the recipient of the PCN may appeal against the authority's decision to an adjudicator;

---

68 S.I. 2007/3483, Schedule 1, Paragraph 2

- the recipient of the PCN may, by notice in writing to the enforcement authority, request it to make available at one of its offices specified by him/her, free of charge and at a time during normal office hours so specified, for viewing by him/her or by his/her representative, the record of the contravention produced by an approved device pursuant to which the penalty charge was imposed; or to provide him/her, free of charge, with such still images from that record as, in the authority's opinion, establish the contravention.

8.85 **It is recommended that the PCN also gives:**

- **vehicle make and colour (if evident);**
- **detailed location of vehicle (full street name);**
- **the contravention code;**
- **observation start and finish times** (where appropriate);
- **PCN number (all PCNs should be uniquely identifiable);**
- amount of penalty time (when relevant).

8.86 **It is recommended that the authority sends a copy of the record of the contravention (in the form of a still image or images) with the PCN.** The authority **must**[69] comply within a reasonable time to requests to see the record of the contravention or send a copy of the still images.

8.87 The regulations set out how authorities **must**[70] calculate the date of service of a postal PCN. Unless proved otherwise, service is taken to have been on the second working date after posting. A working day excludes Saturdays, Sundays, New Year's Day, Good Friday, Christmas Day and any other English bank holidays. The date of posting is not necessarily the same as the date on which the back office staff prepare the PCN. Authorities should make sure that their procedures take account of this.

Immobilisation/removal

8.88 **Very few authorities now use immobilisation. The Secretary of State is of the view that it should only be used in limited circumstances such as where the same vehicle repeatedly breaks parking restrictions and it has not been possible to collect payment for penalties, primarily because the keeper is not registered, or is not properly registered, with the DVLA. Where a vehicle is causing a hazard or obstruction the enforcement authority should remove rather than immobilise. Immobilisation/removal activity should only take place where it gives clear traffic management benefits.**

---

69 S.I. 2007/3482, regulation 3(6)

70 S.I. 2007/3483, regulation 3(2) and regulation 3(3)

8.89 **An enforcement authority should formulate and publish clear guidelines for CEOs on when it will be appropriate to immobilise or remove. The guidelines should cover the order of priority in which vehicles should be dealt with, based on the nature of the contravention. Powers should not be used randomly and authorities should draw up guidelines in consultation with the police.** Immobilisation and removal guidelines should consider the:

- inconvenience that immobilisation causes drivers;
- potential obstruction or loss of parking space that results; and
- effect of immobilisation and removal on public perception and acceptance of CPE.

8.90 Immobilisation and removal are particularly discouraged when it will cause disproportionate inconvenience and potential danger to vulnerable drivers, such as very late at night.

8.91 **The decision on whether to immobilise or to remove a vehicle requires an exercise of judgement and must**[71] **only be taken following specific authorisation by an appropriately trained CEO. The immobilisation/ removal operatives should not take the decision. Vehicles should not be immobilised or removed by contractors unless a suitably trained CEO is present to confirm that the contravention falls within the guidelines.**

8.92 **When a vehicle is parked where parking is permitted, authorities must not**[72] **immobilise or remove in the first 30 minutes following the issuing of the PCN, with the exception of 'persistent evader' vehicles** (see paragraphs 8.105 to 8.107 below) **where the time limit is 15 minutes. When a vehicle has been immobilised, a CEO must**[73] **affix a notice** that says:

- an immobilisation device has been fitted;
- no attempt should be made to drive the vehicle or otherwise put it in motion until it has been released from that device;
- specifying the steps to be taken in order to secure its release; and
- warning that unlawful removal of an immobilisation device is an offence.

8.93 The CEO should attach this notice to the driver's side windscreen or door glass.

8.94 **The immobilisation device may only be removed by or under the direction of a person authorised to do so by the enforcement authority, following payment of the release fee and the penalty charge.**

---

71 S.I. 2007/3483, regulation 13(5)(a) and (b) and The Removal and Disposal of Vehicles Regulations 1986, regulation 5C(2) (inserted by S.I. 2007/3484)

72 The Removal and Disposal of Vehicles Regulations 1986, regulation 5C(2) (inserted by S.I. 2007/3484)

73 S.I. 2007/3483, regulation 12

8.95 Where a vehicle is causing a hazard or obstruction the enforcement authority should remove rather than immobilise. If the vehicle is parked where parking is prohibited (such as on double yellow lines), then the vehicle can be removed as soon as a PCN has been served.[74]

8.96 If a driver returns to the vehicle whilst immobilisation or removal is taking place, then, unless they are a persistent evader, it is recommended that the operation is halted, unless the clamp is secured or the vehicle has all its wheels aboard the tow truck. If immobilisation or removal is halted, the PCN should still be enforced.

8.97 When a vehicle is immobilised and subsequently removed to the pound, the driver does not have to pay the clamp release fee.[75]

8.98 Where vehicles are removed, enforcement authorities should contact the police or, in London, TRACE[76] and advise them of the time, place, vehicle registration number, and pound to attend for retrieval so they can deal with queries from motorists who report their vehicle stolen.

8.99 Where a vehicle has been immobilised or removed, an authority should seek to make it available to its owner immediately upon payment. Authorities should remember that owners have a right to recover their vehicles 24 hours a day. **In the case of clamp release, enforcement authorities should set maximum times for releasing vehicles once they have received payment. They should publish these along with their parking policy guidelines. It is recommended that these should be within one hour from payment being received, with a maximum time limit of two hours. The immobilisation or removal is the penalty and further inconvenience and potential cost from prolonged release times is not appropriate. Enforcement authorities should** measure and **publish their performance against these targets.**

8.100 On the release of a vehicle from a clamp or from the vehicle pound the authority must[77] immediately inform the vehicle owner or person in charge of the vehicle about their right to make representations and their subsequent right to appeal against representations that are rejected. The vehicle will already have been issued a PCN that sets out the grounds on which representations can be made. However, the Secretary of State recommends that the notice about representations against the immobilisation or removal also gives full particulars of the grounds, procedure and time limit for representations. This is particularly important when credit or debit payments are made over the telephone.

---

74 The Removal and Disposal of Vehicles Regulations 1986, regulation 5C(2) (inserted by S.I. 2007/3484)
75 RTRA, section 101A(1) and (3), and TMA, section 79(1)
76 TRACE is operated by the London Councils
77 S.I. 2007/3482, regulation 11(2) and (3), and regulation 8(2) and (3)

8.101 Storage charges should apply for each day or part of day, reckoned from 2400 midnight on the day following removal of a vehicle.

Special consideration for disabled badge holders and vehicles with diplomatic registration plates

8.102 CEOs should be aware of special considerations in respect of valid Blue Badge holders[78] and vehicles with diplomatic plates.[79] See also Chapter 9.

8.103 Vehicles displaying a valid Blue Badge must not[80] be immobilised and, as a general rule, should not be removed. In exceptional circumstances (for example, where a vehicle displaying a Blue Badge is causing a safety hazard), the vehicle should be moved to a safe spot nearby, where possible within sight of its original location. The authorities should not charge a removal fee for the relocation of vehicles displaying a Blue Badge. They should notify the police (in London TRACE) in case the owner reports the vehicle stolen.

8.104 Diplomatic vehicles have registration plates marked with a D or an X, or have personalised plates composed of a country's initials or an abbreviation of its full name. In general, diplomatic vehicles should not be immobilised. The exception is for X registered vehicles which have been identified as persistent evaders. X registered vehicles can be removed but diplomatic vehicles with D or personalised plates that are causing an obstruction or danger should only be repositioned close by as an extreme measure. In such a circumstance, an enforcement authority should not try to recover the costs of removal.

Persistent evaders

8.105 Some vehicle owners contravene parking regulations deliberately and often, and fail to settle the debts they incur. A vehicle owner can be classed as a 'persistent evader' if there are three or more recorded contraventions for the vehicle and the PCNs for these have not been paid, represented against or appealed against within the statutory time limits, or their representations and appeals have been rejected but they have still not paid. Usually this is because the vehicle keeper is not registered, or is not correctly registered, on the DVLA database and the owner is confident that they can avoid paying any penalty charges. An authority should not treat a vehicle owner as a persistent evader unless bailiffs have failed to recoup the outstanding and unchallenged penalty charges. **Where a vehicle appears**

---

[78] see DfT's Blue Badge scheme leaflet *Parking concessions* for disabled and blind people

[79] Article 31.1 of the Vienna Convention on Diplomatic Relations; Diplomatic Privileges Act 1964; White Paper on Diplomatic Immunities and Privileges (Cmnd 9497, April 1985)

[80] S.I. 2007/3483, regulation 13 (1)

to be registered in the UK, but the identity and address is not registered, or is not correctly registered on the DVLA database, authorities should consider making the information available to the police who can, if appropriate, investigate any criminal offence.

8.106 When parked in contravention, a persistent evader's vehicle should be subject to the strongest possible enforcement following the issue of the PCN and confirmation of persistent evader status. This is likely to involve immobilisation or removal. The benefit of removal is that it requires proof of ownership and a registered address before release of the vehicle, whereas immobilisation prevents law abiding motorists from using valuable kerb space. If a vehicle of a persistent evader is in a designated parking place, the Traffic Management Act 2004 and regulations made under it prohibit an enforcement authority from immobilisation or removing the vehicle until at least 15 minutes[81] have elapsed following the issue of a PCN. Currently, under TMA regulations an authority can only obtain payment for the PCN of the contravention for which the vehicle is immobilised or removed and not any other outstanding PCNs.

8.107 London Councils has set up a persistent evader database and all English authorities may use it. Alternatively, authorities may wish to maintain a database themselves, or in conjunction with neighbouring authorities.

---

81 TMA, section 79 (6); S.I. 2007/3483, regulation 13(5)(a); The Removal and Disposal of Vehicles Regulations 1986, regulation 5C(4)(a) (inserted by S.I. 2007/3484)

CHAPTER 9
Exemptions, waivers and dispensations

9.1 Authorities should take account of the exemptions, waivers and dispensations set out below when formulating their parking and enforcement policies and adopt those that are required.

Blue Badge (disabled persons parking) Scheme

9.2 section 49A of the Disability Discrimination Act 1995 (DDA), as inserted by section 3 of the Disability Discrimination Act 2005, requires (among other things) that all public authorities, in carrying out their functions, must have due regard to:

- eliminate discrimination and harassment that is unlawful under the DDA;
- the need to promote equality of opportunity between disabled persons and others; and
- the need to provide for people with disabilities, even if that involves treating disabled persons more favourably.

9.3 The Secretary of State attaches particular importance to catering for older and disabled people. Around 10 per cent of the adult population has some form of disability, and taking other factors into account, many more people have some sort of mobility problem. It is therefore an important part of Government policy that disabled people or those with mobility problems should be able to travel with the minimum of difficulty.

9.4 The Blue Badge Scheme provides a range of national on-street parking concessions for disabled people, with severe mobility problems, who have difficulty using public transport. The Scheme is designed to help severely disabled people to travel independently, as either a driver or passenger, by allowing them to park close to their destination. However, the Blue Badge scheme concessions do not apply to four central London boroughs:

- City of London;
- City of Westminster;
- Royal Borough of Kensington and Chelsea; and
- part of the London Borough of Camden.

9.5 The parking concessions available to Blue Badge[82] holders continue to apply automatically when civil parking enforcement is introduced. The regulations broadly require that all TROs should exempt Blue Badge holders, allowing them to park:

- free of charge and without time limit at on-street parking meters and pay-and-display spaces;
- as long as they wish where others may park only for a limited time, unless there is an Order in place specifically time-limiting parking for Blue Badge holders; and
- on single or double yellow lines for up to three hours except where there is a ban on loading and unloading.

9.6 Blue Badge holders, like other road users, must obey the Highway Code. For example, they are not entitled to park:

- in loading bays during the hours of operation;
- on pedestrian crossings (including zigzag area);
- on bus stop clearways; and
- on school 'keep clear' markings during hours of operation.

9.7 They should also not park where it would endanger, inconvenience or obstruct pedestrians or other road users. This includes on a bend, close to a junction or where the kerb has been lowered or the road raised for wheelchair users. You can find further information in the DfT booklet *The Blue Badge Scheme: rights and responsibilities*.[83]

9.8 Vehicles displaying a valid Blue Badge **must not**[84] be immobilised in CEAs. This recognises the difficulties which many disabled people would have in getting to a payments centre and the risk of injury or undue suffering if forced to wait for their vehicle to be released. Police constables and enforcement officers (such as traffic wardens and civil enforcement officers) have the power to inspect Blue Badges.[85]

9.9 Holders of a valid Blue Badge do not have statutory exemption from removal action as they do from clamping. However, disabled people frequently rely heavily or completely upon their vehicles and removal can cause them great inconvenience. The Secretary of State recommends that vehicles displaying a valid Blue Badge are only removed if there is an emergency, security or ceremonial reason, or the vehicle is causing a serious safety hazard or obstruction.

---

82 Local Authorities' Traffic Orders (Exemptions for Disabled Persons) (England) Regulations 2000 (SI 2000/683).

83 available quoting ref T/INF/1214 from DfT Free Literature. Tel: 0870 1226 236

84 TMA, section 79(5)

85 TMA, section 94

9.10   If removal of a vehicle displaying a Blue Badge is absolutely necessary and the driver cannot be found within a reasonable time, the police move the vehicle to a position nearby where it will not cause a hazard or obstruction. Whenever possible, they leave a message for the driver telling, them where the vehicle is. The Secretary of State recommends that authorities do the same.

Abuse of the Blue Badge scheme

9.11   There are several ways in which Blue Badges can be misused. These include:

- use of a badge that is no longer valid;
- misuse of a valid badge by a friend or relative, with or without the badge holder's knowledge or permission;
- use by the holder of a badge that has been reported lost or stolen – possibly to obtain another badge for a friend or relation; and
- use of a stolen or copied badge by the thief, forger or someone who has acquired it from them.

Targeted surveillance operations

9.12   The most common form of abuse tends to be misuse of the badge by the friends and family of the holder. Where this is a clear problem (and there is a business case for tackling it) DfT strongly recommends that authorities set up a specialist Blue Badge enforcement team to carry out undercover surveillance work. The team can identify suspected systematic abuse and apply for permission to carry out undercover surveillance[86] in order to build up evidence that can later be used to prosecute the individual in the Magistrates Court.

Working with the police

9.13   Local enforcement teams may identify Blue Badge abuse 'hot spots', such as those around football stadiums, schools, shopping centres or entertainment/sports facilities. Under the power to inspect legislation (see text box below) parking enforcement officials have powers to inspect badges, but only police officers have the power to seize and confiscate lost, stolen, fraudulent, invalid or misused badges. Inspection swoops by local authorities and the police on hot spot areas can have a big impact on levels of badge abuse.

Day-to-day enforcement inspections

9.14   Parking enforcement officers play an important part in identifying lost, stolen and fraudulent badges. Whenever a CEO suspects misuse or abuse of a badge, they need to deal with the badge holder in a sensitive manner. They should not make any assumption or ask any questions about why the holder has been issued with a badge, as this is not the enforcement officer's role. In addition, some disabilities may not be immediately visible. We strongly recommend that enforcement officers receive disability awareness training.

---

86   Regulation of Investigatory Powers Act 2000 (RIPA)

9.15 From 15 October 2007, a gender marker has been added to the TSO serial number, prefixed by an 'x' for male badge holders and a 'y' for female. The marker has been added to help identify obvious cases of misuse.

9.16 Authorised officers can check the badge through the windscreen and, if necessary, ask to see it under the 'power to inspect' (see below). They can then check the detailed information and verify the photograph of the badge holder on the back.

Power to inspect

section 94 of the Traffic Management Act 2004 introduced the 'power to inspect' Blue Badges for police officers, traffic wardens, local authority parking attendants and civil enforcement officers ('authorised officers' as defined in section 76 of the Act).

This Act makes it an offence for an individual to fail to produce a badge when asked to by any of these authorised persons. However, this power can only legally be exercised when a person is in the vehicle or when they are leaving or returning to a vehicle displaying a badge.

Only a police officer has the power to seize a Blue Badge where it is required as evidence in a criminal prosecution, so authorities often need to work in partnership with the police.

9.17 Table 9.1 summarises the powers available to tackle different types of Blue Badge abuse. You can find detailed guidance on the enforcement of the Scheme in DfT's *The Blue Badge Scheme Local Authority Guidance (England).*[87]

Table 9.1 Summary of powers available to tackle different types of Blue Badge abuse

Abuse	Application	Powers	Relevant legislation
Acquisition of badge by false representation	Where a badge holder provided false information in order to qualify for a badge.	Local authority can require return of the badge if they are satisfied that it has been obtained by false representation.	Regulation 9(2)(b) of the Disabled Persons (Badges for Motor Vehicles) (England) Regulations 2000 (SI 2000/682)
Misuse of badge in certain circumstances	Where a badge holder is using a badge for which they no longer qualify due to a change in their circumstances. Where a badge holder is using an expired badge. Where a badge holder is using a badge which is no longer legible.	If found guilty, person could face fine of up to £1,000 on conviction. Authority could issue a Fixed Penalty Notice or a Penalty Charge Notice if a parking offence has occurred. The police can also seize the badge as evidence.	Section 21 (4B) of the Chronically Sick and Disabled Persons Act 1970. Parking offences under the Road Traffic Regulation Act 1984 Section 19 of the Police and Criminal Evidence Act 1984 (general power of seizure etc.).

---

87 January 2008

Abuse	Application	Powers	Relevant legislation
Systematic misuse of valid badge by holder	Where a badge holder or other person using a badge with the holder's consent has misused the badge, leading to at least three relevant convictions.	Local authority can withdraw a badge and require its return (on account of its misuse leading to at least three relevant convictions). Authority could issue Fixed Penalty Notice or a Penalty Charge Notice if a parking offence has occurred.	Regulation 9(2)(a) of the Disabled Persons (Badges for Motor Vehicles) (England) Regulations 2000 (SI 2007/682). Parking offences under the Road Traffic Regulation Act 1984.
Misuse of badge by a non-badge holder	Where a non badge holder is using a badge (with or without the badge holder's permission) and the badge holder is not present.	If found guilty, person could face a fine of £1,000 on conviction. Authority could issue a Fixed Penalty Notice or a Penalty Charge Notice if a parking offence has occurred. The police can also seize the badge as evidence.	Section 117 of the Road Traffic Regulation Act 1984. Parking offences under the Road Traffic Regulation Act 1984. section 19 of the Police and Criminal Evidence Act 1984 (general power of seizure etc).
Refusal to produce a badge for inspection when requested by an authorised person	Where the police or enforcement officer has asked to inspect the badge. This can include instances where they believe the badge has been stolen, forged, fraudulently altered or is not being used by the badge holder.	The police and enforcement officers have the power to inspect badges when displayed on the vehicle and a person is either in the vehicle, or appears to have been in or is about to get into the vehicle. It is an offence for a badge holder without reasonable excuse to fail to produce a badge when asked and a person can be fined up to £1,000 if convicted. The police can also seize the badge as evidence.	Section 21(4ba) of the chronically sick and disabled persons act 1970. Section 21(4bd) of the chronically sick and disabled persons act 1970. Section 19 of the police and Criminal Evidence Act 1984 (general power of seizure etc.).

Withdrawing badges due to repeated misuse

9.18 Local authorities can withdraw a badge if the holder has had at least three relevant convictions for misuse.[88] Local Authorities can also request the return of a badge if they are satisfied that it was falsely obtained.

9.19 DfT strongly recommends that authorities should issue a warning notice to a badge holder who is misusing a badge, or allowing their badge to be misused, before considering withdrawing the badge.

Reciprocal arrangements for disabled drivers from other countries

9.20 Following the introduction of a common European disabled persons' parking card (the Blue Badge), the UK now has reciprocal arrangements with all European Union Member States. These give badge holders the right to parking concessions provided in the host country by displaying a badge issued under their own national scheme.

9.21 CEOs should treat vehicles displaying the Blue Badge of a participating country as if it were displaying a UK Blue Badge. However, the concessions that badge holders are entitled to vary from country to country.[89]

9.22 If a vehicle displays a Blue Badge equivalent from a country without reciprocal arrangements, then the Blue Badge exemptions need not apply unless the local authority has agreed to recognise badges from that country. However, the general obligation in the DDA still applies if a vehicle is believed to be used by a disabled person. Enforcement authorities should take great care to ensure that they meet their obligations.

Diplomatic registered vehicles

9.23 Special arrangements apply to diplomatic registered vehicles. Authorities should accurately follow the procedures used by the police when dealing with diplomatic registered vehicles. Where a CEO comes across a diplomatically registered vehicle parked in contravention of a parking restriction, they should contact a manager or supervisor who should follow the procedures set out below.

9.24 Diplomatic registered vehicles will have one of three types of plate:

- **D registration plates** (e.g. 123 D 321) may be carried by vehicles belonging to diplomats, members of the administrative and technical staff of missions and certain senior staff of international organisations. They may also be carried by official vehicles of diplomatic missions. They show that the owner is entitled to diplomatic immunity;

---

88 Disabled Persons (Badges for Motor Vehicles) (England) (Amendment) Regulations 2000 – section 9(2)

89 *European Parking Card for People with Disabilities – How, When and Where to Use it in 29 Countries* available at: http://www.iam.org.uk/motoringtrust/advice/parking/bluebadgeuserparkingineurope.htm

- **Personalised diplomatic registration plates** may, for example, indicate a country's initials or an abbreviation of its full name. They are sometimes issued for the official cars of Heads of Diplomatic Missions, who have full diplomatic immunity; or

- **X registration plates** (e.g. 987 X 789) may be used by certain consular staff or staff of international organisations. They show that the owner is entitled to limited diplomatic immunity.

9.25   The UK is a party to Article 31.1 of the Vienna Convention on Diplomatic Relations, which gives accredited diplomats immunity from the criminal jurisdiction of the host nation's law. The Article is given the force of law in the United Kingdom by section 2 of, and Schedule 1 to, the Diplomatic Privileges Act 1964. Issuing PCNs is not considered an exercise of criminal jurisdiction within the terms of Article 31.1 of the Convention, nor is the removal of diplomatic vehicles **as a last resort** to relieve obstruction or danger when the driver cannot be found quickly. However, immobilising or removing those vehicles in other circumstances is considered to be an exercise of such jurisdiction and is therefore ruled out. The White Paper on Diplomatic Immunities and Privileges[90] commits the Government to ensuring that agencies enforcing parking controls follow these principles.

9.26   The TMA provides for non-endorsable parking contraventions to be enforceable by local authorities in a Civil Enforcement Area. But the immobilisation or removal of vehicles sometimes associated with the enforcement of these controls still constitutes the exercise of criminal jurisdiction within the meaning of the Vienna Convention. The Diplomatic Privileges Act 1964 continues to exempt diplomatic vehicles from such enforcement.

Immobilisation

9.27   Authorities should not immobilise vehicles carrying 'D' registration plates or registration plates personalised for the country anywhere on public roads. Vehicles carrying X registration plates **may** be immobilised in the same way as vehicles without diplomatic immunity and authorities may require owners or persons in charge of such vehicles to pay the PCN and a release fee. However, the Secretary of State recommends that local authorities treat X-plated vehicles as D-plated unless they are persistent evaders. Authorities should never immobilise an X-plated vehicle where it is parked if it is causing a serious road safety or congestion hazard, even if they could justify doing so. They should move it to a place nearby or take it to the vehicle pound.

Removal

9.28   Authorities should only remove vehicles carrying D registration plates or registration plates personalised for the country **as a last resort** to relieve obstruction or danger to other road users and where the driver cannot be found quickly. In these cases, the vehicle should be removed to a

---

[90]   Cmnd 9497, April 1985

more suitable location within the immediate vicinity and, where possible, a message left indicating where it can be found. Authorities should avoid moving vehicles to a car pound but if there is no viable alternative, charges should be waived as diplomats are under no obligation to pay removal or storage charges. If an authority does demand a charge and it is paid, the Embassy will appeal to the Foreign and Commonwealth Office (FCO) to recover the charges, or will appeal direct to the authority.

9.29 As with immobilisation, authorities may remove vehicles carrying X registration plates in the same way as those without any diplomatic immunity, and require the owners to pay the PCN and any associated removal, storage and disposal charges. The Secretary of State recommends that authorities treat X-plated vehicles as D-plated unless they are causing a serious road safety or congestion hazard or are persistent evaders.

Recovery of unpaid PCNs

9.30 Although the owners of diplomatic registered vehicles are required to pay PCNs, authorities should not serve an NtO if they do not pay within 28 days. The NtO would trigger procedures which could ultimately lead to action in a county court to recover the unpaid debt. Many diplomats are not subject to civil jurisdiction and there is no practical way for local authorities to distinguish between those who are and those who are not. Local authorities should therefore follow existing police practice. Instead of issuing an NtO, they should record the unpaid charge. The FCO will ask for details of all unpaid PCNs annually and will pursue the contraveners for payment.

9.31 The Government may ask for diplomats who persistently disregard the controls and refuse to pay the penalties to be withdrawn from duty in the United Kingdom. The FCO will also report once a year to Parliament on the number of outstanding PCNs issued in respect of diplomatically registered vehicles and break down the contraveners by country.

9.32 Authorities should send details of the appropriate contact in the authority to the FCO so they can collect information each year about the outstanding penalties in respect of diplomatically registered vehicles. Details should be sent to:

Team 1
Diplomatic Missions and International Organisations Unit
Protocol Directorate
Room 1/61
Old Admiralty Building
London
SW1A 2AH

Telephone 020 7008 0975

Application to HM forces and visiting forces

9.33 When a local authority is given CPE powers, they **must not** use them against any vehicles[91] that:

- are being used or appropriated for use by HM forces; or
- belong to, or at the relevant time is being used or appropriated for use by visiting forces (such as the United States Visiting Forces).

9.34 These vehicles will generally bear identification plates rather than registration plates. This is because they are not required to be registered under regulations made under the Vehicle Excise and Registration Act 1994. The net effect is that vehicles used by Her Majesty's army, navy and air force, or vehicles used by visiting armed forces, will not be subject to civil parking controls in CEAs.

Waivers

9.35 There are some circumstances where vehicles need to be parked in such a way that they cannot comply with the regulations, for example removal vehicles or scaffolding lorries. Authorities should issue special waivers (also called dispensations) to allow these vehicles to park without attracting penalties. It is important that authorities establish their own policies and procedures for granting waivers and provide for them in their TROs. Policies need to balance the importance to businesses of accessible parking in special circumstances with the need to keep roads clear, and ensure that the use of waivers is not excessive.

Dispensations for professional care workers

9.36 The London Health Emergency Badge (HEB) scheme allows doctors, nurses, midwives and health visitors engaged in urgent or emergency health care in (but not routine visits to) a patient's home to park where there is no alternative:

- without payment;
- in residents' or other reserved parking bays; and
- on yellow lines where loading and unloading is not prohibited (as long as there in not a serious obstruction or other endorseable offence).

9.37 Enforcement authorities should consult with health trust(s) in their area about introducing a similar scheme that permits parking by professional health care workers making emergency or urgent health calls in areas where controls are in force. If an authority does not provide such a scheme the health trust may be unable to provide the public with these services. Authorities should tell professional health care workers in their areas about any permit scheme they plan to introduce before civil parking enforcement begins. They should also tell them about any subsequent changes to the arrangements.

---

91 TMA section 90

9.38 The Secretary of State recommends a number of conditions to help prevent abuse of such a scheme. The authority should issue health workers with badges, signed by the badge holder and a council official. The badge should show:

- its purpose, for example 'Waiting and loading and designated parking place orders: waiver – consent to park and conditions imposed';
- the name of the issuing local authority;
- the name and contact details of the badge holder (if appropriate);[92]
- the registration number of the vehicle (if appropriate);[93]
- that the vehicle should be moved on the instructions of a police officer, traffic warden or CEO; and
- the expiry date.

9.39 The badge should be displayed on or inside the windscreen so that it can be seen clearly from outside. It should only be used when the badge holder is away from his or her base and directly involved in patient care, and where there are no legal parking places available.

9.40 If a CEO suspects misuse of the badge, they may issue a PCN or the vehicle may be immobilised or removed. A vehicle displaying a valid badge should not normally be immobilised, removed or served with a PCN before an attempt is made to contact the driver at the address shown on the badge. If frequent or regular misuse occurs, the authority may withdraw the badge. Dispensations do not apply if the vehicle is causing a serious obstruction or has been left for an excessive time in the same place.

Exemptions where parking places are suspended

9.41 Authorities may suspend parking places for a number of reasons. TROs may permit certain vehicles to park in suspended places (for example, cranes and lorries where a bay is suspended for building work or highway maintenance; vans for furniture removals; hearses for funerals). Similarly, TROs may allow parking bays to be reserved for a doctor, Blue Badge holder, diplomat or resident, if that person's usual parking bay is suspended. Such exemptions are a matter for local authorities. However, it is important that suspended and reserved parking bays are clearly signed, so that motorists can easily see whether and when they are permitted to park there.

---

[92] In London the HEB is issued to the practice to be shared among staff who need to use it rather than to a specific individual or vehicle. There is space for the user to enter on the badge the address they are visiting

[93] *Ibid*

Miscellaneous exemptions

9.42 TROs invariably exempt vehicles being used for fire service, ambulance or police purposes, or being used to remove an obstruction (such as a broken down vehicle). TROs usually also exempt service vehicles, but only when they are being used to carry out certain activities (for example, telecommunications vehicles when laying lines, or vehicles of a universal postal service provider delivering mail). These are not general exemptions for vehicles of a certain type, irrespective of use.

9.43 Drivers of vehicles benefiting from such exemptions should already know which parking controls they are exempt from. CEOs should also know the local exemptions so they do not issue PCNs. The exact extent of exemptions will depend on the precise terms of the traffic order.

CHAPTER 10
Policy and administrative functions

Providing a quality service

10.1 Enforcement authorities should make sure that their processes for recovering outstanding penalties and handling challenges, representations and appeals are efficient, effective and impartial. Processes must comply with all relevant primary legislation, regulations, traffic regulation orders and local byelaws. Authorities are encouraged to seek independent quality assurance of their CPE processes. Authorities should use IT systems that facilitate speedy and accurate processes.

10.2 Enforcement authorities should deal with motorists promptly and professionally. Authorities are encouraged to set time and quality targets for dealing with queries, in addition to any statutory time limits and those set out in the Statutory Guidance. They should report on performance against these targets in their annual report. Enforcement authorities must[94] use first class post for any notice or Charge Certificate.

10.3 Authorities should remember that an appeal is a judicial proceeding and that time limits for correspondence may be laid down in legislation or set using adjudicator's judicial powers. Authorities are advised to respond promptly to contacts from the adjudicator concerning appeals.

10.4 Enforcement authorities should offer motorists flexible and efficient ways to contact them, including e-mail and telephone. They should ensure there is an adequate audit trail to rebut any accusations of unfairness.

Collecting penalty charges

10.5 The penalty charge is usually payable by the owner[95] of the vehicle, unless the vehicle was hired at the time of the contravention.

---

94 S.I. 2007/3483, regulation 3 (4)

95 This expression is defined by the Traffic Management Act 2004 section 92 as follows: 'owner', in relation to a vehicle, means the person by whom the vehicle is kept, which in the case of a vehicle registered under the Vehicle Excise and Registration Act 1994 (c. 22) is presumed (unless the contrary is proved) to be the person in whose name the vehicle is registered.

10.6 No criminal proceedings may be instituted and no Fixed Penalty Notice may be served in respect of any parking contravention occurring in a CEA except to enforce a prohibition on vehicles stopping on or near pedestrian crossings.[96] If the enforcement authority and the police both take enforcement action, the criminal action takes precedence and the PCN must be cancelled. If the PCN has already been paid, the authority **must**[97] refund it.

10.7 The successful introduction of civil parking enforcement requires convenient and up-to-date facilities for the payment of penalty and other parking charges. Motorists may be more likely to pay penalty charges if it is quick and easy to do so. Vehicles that have been immobilised or removed should be returned to the owner as soon as possible. An efficient and secure system for collecting penalty charge revenue will improve an authority's financial performance by minimising bad debts and the time-consuming and costly actions needed to collect them.

10.8 **Enforcement authorities should offer motorists a range of facilities for paying penalty charges. Where they provide payment centres these should be safe and accessible.** Payment centres should be an integral part of the system for processing PCNs, so that the financial transactions can be recorded immediately and any further action cancelled. **Enforcement authorities should ensure that any payment facility (particularly telephone and online payments) can confirm any amount outstanding if part payment only has been received.**

10.9 The choice of payment methods for penalty and other charges needs to balance ease of settlement for the motorist with security of payment and cost-effectiveness for the authority. The range of payment methods should reflect the scale of each authority's enforcement operations, including the number of penalty charges to be collected and payments arising from any vehicle immobilisation or removal operations.

10.10 It is important that authorities do not introduce a system that inadvertently discriminates against some sections of the population. The system should allow motorists to pay by whatever method is most convenient to them, including:

- cash;
- cheque sent by post without cheque guarantee card;
- cheque supported by a cheque guarantee card presented at a payments centre;
- Sterling travellers' cheque; and
- debit or credit card, in person, by phone or via the internet.

---

96 TMA – Schedule 7 paragraphs 3 (2)(c) and (h)(i), and 4(2)(c) and (i)(i)
97 S.I. 2007/3483, regulation 7

10.11 If a penalty is paid or purports to have been paid and is later withdrawn or cancelled the time in which enforcement action may be taken is extended – see paragraph 10.37.[98]

10.12 Some cheques received through the post will inevitably be made out to the wrong payee (for example, to a neighbouring authority). If this happens regularly, authorities may wish to consider establishing a payment exchange. Cheques endorsed 'A/C Payee Only' and 'Not Negotiable' – terms which are invariably pre-printed on company cheques and often on personal cheques – cannot be made over to other parties. An authority could return a cheque endorsed in this way to the drawer. An authority could either return it directly, if they know the address, or via the drawer's bank, with an instruction to make it payable to the correct payee. Alternatively, the authority could transfer the cheque to the named payee, in return for a cheque for a corresponding sum made payable to it.

10.13 It is important that authorities deal with any misdirected cheques promptly and write to drawers explaining how their cheques have been handled and why. They should not acknowledge unsecured cheques until they have cleared. It may be helpful to advise people sending payment through the post to record key details (PCN or car registration number) on the back of the cheque to minimise the risk of matching errors.

10.14 Authorities will need procedures to deal with cases where payment is made within the discount period but subject to 'conditions' or in envelopes that are not stamped. It may be better to refuse payments made on conditions.

10.15 Authorities will also need to establish procedures for dealing with overpayments, underpayments and unidentified payments. Enforcement authorities should credit unidentified payments to the correct PCN record as soon as possible.

10.16 Where a local authority is immobilising or removing vehicles, the amount which a motorist will need to pay, allowing for the outstanding penalty charge, may exceed the limit of a cheque guarantee or debit card. The conditions governing their use may state that the bank only guarantees payment of a single transaction up to the card limit. Accepting a series of payments up to the card limit is considered fraudulent use of the card, and banks could return the second and subsequent cheques unpaid. A more secure payment method than a partially secured cheque will therefore minimise bad debts.

10.17 Paying by online debit and credit cards is convenient for many motorists and is more secure for local authorities. The electronic card readers automatically seeks authorisation for values previously agreed between the card holder and the card company, and automatically bars any 'blacklisted' cards. Auditors favour the use of online debit and credit cards to avoid creating bad debts and minimising collection costs. There are operational savings to debit/credit cards so authorities cannot justify applying surcharges for their use.

---

98 S.I. 2007/3483, regulation 20 (2)(c)

10.18 Payment of a penalty charge by credit or debit card on the telephone or over the internet has many advantages for authorities and for motorists. It is particularly effective for collecting release fees for immobilised vehicles. The card holder can give authority to debit the account by telephone, subject to the agreement of the credit or debit card companies. It may be worth reminding motorists that even if they do not have internet access at home, they can make payments from a local library or internet café. There may be a case for providing a terminal in the authority's customer contact centre or (if they have one) parking shop.

10.19 Authorities which see significant numbers of foreign visitors may wish to take payment in foreign currency, particularly for immobilisation or removal. They should use a bureau de change to quote the day's exchange rate. It may be more difficult to detect forged foreign currency. Authorities also need to consider who will pay any currency conversion charges. Visitors may claim that they have been unfairly penalised if they are asked to pay the conversion charge, but the authority might otherwise risk becoming a cost-effective way for residents to exchange unused foreign currency.

10.20 **A PCN is deemed 'paid' as soon as the payment arrives at any payment office belonging to the enforcement authority that issued the PCN. Whether this is the parking payment office or another payment office, the enforcement authority should promptly close the case. An authority's systems should accurately record the day on which it receives payments so that no further enforcement action is taken.**

10.21 **If there are unusual delays with the postal system, authorities should make allowances for late payments made by post when considering whether a payment was received within the statutory period. Enforcement authorities may wish to keep the envelope that the payments came in, as the franking can be used as evidence of the date of posting.**

10.22 **Where the enforcement authority receives full payment within 14 days of the service of the PCN, it must[99] accept the discounted amount. Unless the Secretary of State authorises a departure from the guidelines on the levels of penalty charges, the discount must be set at the applicable discount – currently 50 per cent of the penalty charge.[100] The authority should then close the case. When a PCN has been served by post using evidence from an approved device, the discount period is 21 days from the date of service of the notice.[101]**

---

99 S.I. 2007/3483, Schedule, regulation 1(h)

100 S.I. 2007/3487

101 S.I. 2007/3483, Schedule, regulation 3(a)

Location of payment centres and opening hours

10.23 Where immobilisation and removals are not part of an authority's enforcement regime, most motorists are likely to pay by phone, post and, when possible, on-line. Where a motorist wishes to pay in person it may be most efficient to provide payment facilities at a town hall, civic centre or other places where the public makes payments to the local authority. Alternatively, where a contractor is being used, it may be possible to allow payment where enforcement operations are based. Enforcement without immobilisation or vehicle removals does not deprive a motorist of the use of his or her vehicle, so there is less need for payment centres to be open outside normal office hours. However, authorities may wish to consider extending opening hours if this is likely to encourage prompt payment.

10.24 Where an authority immobilises or removes vehicles, it is particularly important that payment methods are convenient and accessible. A payment centre should be an integral part of the pound to which vehicles are removed, so that motorists can pay the charges and reclaim their vehicle at the same time. If the vehicle pound is inconveniently situated, the authority should provide one or more payment centres in or near the areas where immobilisation commonly occurs for motorists who wish to pay release fees in person rather than over the phone.

10.25 The vehicle pound payment centre and any payment centre intended primarily for paying immobilisation charges should be open during the hours that immobilisation and removal take place. If this is not feasible, they should be open between 8am and midnight, Monday to Saturday, and between 9am and 5pm on Sundays and public holidays. Longer opening hours may be necessary at certain times, such as summer weekends and bank holidays at seaside resorts. There should also be an out of hours emergency service. Authorities will need to coordinate payment and release procedures to ensure that vehicles can always be released a reasonable time after payment (see Chapter 8).

Temporary waiving of payments

10.26 There will be circumstances where a motorist will be unable to pay the charges to release his or her vehicle from an immobilisation device or pound, but there are strong compassionate grounds for releasing the vehicle. For example, the person reclaiming the vehicle is a vulnerable person with no immediate means of payment and it is late at night. Local authorities should formulate policies for the release of vehicles in such circumstances. Before releasing the vehicle, the authority should ask the motorist to sign a promissory note to pay the outstanding debt.

10.27 One way to minimise bad debts where vehicles are released on compassionate grounds is to accept part payments on the spot. It is arguable that accepting part payment would make the recovery of small debts uneconomic and the practice could become an 'unofficial discount'. On the other hand, whilst debt recovery through the County Court is unlikely to prove economic if viewed in isolation, the deterrent effect of instigating proceedings to recover all bad debts may keep non-payment levels down and outweigh the cost of proceedings.

10.28 Authorities that decide to accept part payments should first seek payment of immobilisation, removal, storage or disposal charges. This is because unpaid penalty charges can be recovered using less expensive procedures.

10.29 In cases of proven hardship, local authorities may wish to consider allowing outstanding penalty or other charges to be paid in instalments.

Payments for release of a vehicle from an immobilisation device or a vehicle pound

10.30 After full or part payment or the waiving of the appropriate charges, the release of a vehicle from an immobilisation device or vehicle pound should be properly documented. The motorist **must** immediately be given written advice about their rights to make representations and, if that is rejected, an appeal[102] and the grounds upon which they can be made.

10.31 Many motorists whose vehicles have been immobilised will pay the release fee by phone rather than at a payment centre. Authorities will need to establish procedures for handling payments and issuing written advice about representations and appeals that comply with the law.

Issuing the Notice to Owner

10.32 **If the penalty charge is not paid the enforcement authority may issue a Notice to Owner (NtO). The purpose of the NtO is to ensure that the PCN was received by the vehicle owner and to remind the vehicle owner that the PCN is now due to be paid in full and if it is not paid within a further 28 days it may be increased** – currently by 50 per cent. It also gives the owner an opportunity to make formal representations against the penalty charge. **The NtO may be issued 28 days after serving the PCN, and we expect authorities to send them within 56 days after serving the PCN. The ultimate time limit, in exceptional circumstances, is six months**[103] **from the 'relevant date'. There should be a very good reason for waiting that long to serve a notice to owner.** The relevant date is usually the date on which the PCN was served. It may also be the date on which:

- a district judge serves written notice in response to a witness statement;
- an earlier NtO relating to the contravention is cancelled in response to representations; or
- the authority is notified that payment (or purported payment) of a PCN has been cancelled or withdrawn.

---

102 S.I. 2007/3482, Part 3
103 S.I. 2007/3482, regulation 20

10.33 The NtO **must**[104] state:

- the date of the notice, which must be the date on which the notice is posted;
- the name of the enforcement authority serving the notice;
- the amount of the penalty charge payable;
- the date on which the PCN was served;
- The grounds on which the CEO who served the PCN under regulation 9 believed that a penalty charge was payable with respect to the vehicle;
- that the penalty charge, if not already paid, must be paid within the period of 28 days beginning with the date on which the notice is served (the payment period);
- that if, after the payment period has expired, no representations have been made under regulation 4 of SI 2007/3482 (regulation 4) and the penalty charge has not been paid, the enforcement authority may increase the penalty charge by the applicable surcharge – currently 50 per cent;
- the amount of the increased penalty charge;
- that representations on the basis specified in regulation 4 against payment of the penalty charge may be made to the enforcement authority, but that any representations made outside the payment period may be disregarded;
- the nature of the representations which may be made under regulation 4;
- the address (including if appropriate any e-mail address or fax telephone number as well as the postal address) to which representations must be sent;
- the form in which representations must be made;
- that if representations which have been made within the payment period, or outside the payment period but not disregarded, are not accepted by the enforcement authority the recipient of the notice may appeal against the authority's decision to an adjudicator; and
- In general terms, the form and manner in which an appeal may be made.

10.34 The regulations set out how the date of service of an NtO **must**[105] be calculated. Unless proved otherwise, service is taken to have been on the second working date after posting. A working day excludes a Saturday, a Sunday, New Year's Day, Good Friday, Christmas Day and any other English bank holiday. The date of posting is not necessarily the same as the date on which the back office staff prepare the NtO, and authorities should make sure that their procedures take account of this.

10.35 **There are different requirements when the PCN** has been served by post and so **acts as the NtO** (see Chapter 8).

---

104 S.I. 2007/3483, regulation 19(2) and S.I. 2007/3482, regulation 3(3)
105 S.I. 2007/3483, regulation 3(2) and regulation 3(3)

10.36 Authorities must[106] specify on the NtO (or PCN when served by post) the statutory grounds on which representations may be made. Where a photograph or other camera evidence shows that the parking contravention took place, authorities should send this with the NtO, as it should help to prevent unfounded representations.

10.37 If payment of a penalty charge has been made or has been purported to have been made (for example by cheque or credit card) and the payment has been cancelled after the limitation period has expired, the regulations permit the enforcement authority to serve an NtO.[107]

Information from DVLA about the registered keeper

10.38 In order to issue an NtO, the enforcement authority will need to know the name and address of the registered keeper of the vehicle at the time the unpaid PCN was served. Authorities can get this information from DVLA.[108] Parking contractors may approach DVLA direct for this information, provided that each request is supported by a letter of authority from the enforcement authority on whose behalf they are working. The letter must never be dated more than three months before the request is made.

10.39 Authorities preparing their applications to enforce civil parking should contact DVLA at an early stage to discuss methods of transmitting data and other technical requirements.[109] They should also check whether the IT provider they propose to use already has a DVLA interface.

10.40 An authority should request the name and address of the registered keeper from DVLA at least seven days before the NtO is due to be served. For each unpaid PCN, the local authority needs to provide DVLA with the vehicle registration number and the date of the contravention. Requests may be submitted via dedicated, secure electronic links or established paper channels. DVLA tries to process data sent by electronic link during the following night if received before 5pm. Requests processed during the night will usually be returned by 7 am the next day.

10.41 The information returned to a local authority in response to each request will comprise:

- vehicle registration mark (that is, number plate);
- name and address of the registered keeper;
- date for which the results are provided;
- vehicle make, mode and colour; and

---

106 S.I. 2007/3483, regulation 19(2) Schedule, Paragraph 2, and S.I. 2007/3482, regulation 3(3) and 3(4).
107 S.I. 2007/3483, regulation 20(2)(c)
108 Non-fee paying enquiries, Driver and Vehicle Licensing Agency (DVLA), Longview Road, Swansea SA6 7JL
109 Queries to Data Sharing and Protection Policy, Policy and External Communications Directorate, DVLA, Longview Road, Swansea, SA6 7JL

- other indicators that the vehicle has been scrapped, stolen, etc (only via the electronic route).

10.42 The information from DVLA should be cross-referenced with the details recorded by the CEO to ensure that the make, model and colour matches that recorded at the roadside. The authority should weed out any recording or keying errors to avoid generating an incorrect NtO.

10.43 The authority will need to check the information it receives from DVLA to identify vehicles which are registered in the name of a corporate body. In these cases, the authority will need to send the NtO specifically to the secretary or clerk of the body corporate and it is unlikely that DVLA will have a record of their name. Where a vehicle is registered in the name of a partnership, the authority can serve the notice on any of the partners at the address which carries out the business. A sole trader is in the same position as any individual, whether or not s/he works under a business name or his or her own name. The authority can send the notice to the sole trader's home or business address.

DVLA record is incomplete

10.44 Where requests for information from DVLA are unsuccessful it may be that the vehicle is a new one and has still to be registered (the vehicle registration number will indicate whether this is likely), or that the new keeper of a used vehicle has not yet notified DVLA. The authority should check whether it sent the correct vehicle details to DVLA and processed the request properly. The authority should send a further request to DVLA with any incorrect details amended. If this second enquiry is unsuccessful, the authority should add details of the vehicle and contravention to its list of 'untraceable owners'. When a vehicle on this list is parked in contravention and has three or more unpaid and unchallenged PCNs recorded against it (see Chapter 8) the authority may immobilise or remove it faster than other vehicles.

10.45 The initial information will be taken from DVLA's vehicle record, but will include a marker to indicate cases where there is an enforcement history file which may contain a more recent address. Where the vehicle record data does not enable a vehicle owner to be traced, the authority will then be able to request name and address details from the enforcement history file. Authorities should note that this information is the last known name and address of the last alleged contravener or (in the case of criminal matters) offender. It should not be taken as confirmation that the current owner is responsible for the outstanding penalties.

10.46 Many authorities currently operating CPE provide DVLA with information about vehicles without a valid VED disc that have been issued with a PCN, thus helping DVLA to track down VED evaders and improve the accuracy of their records. DVLA will establish similar relations with other local authorities preparing to introduce civil parking enforcement. Authorities should contact the Vehicle Customer Services, eVRE section, DVLA, for more details.

Diplomatic vehicles

10.47   Where a PCN is served on a vehicle with a diplomatic registration plate but no payment is received within 28 days, an enforcement authority should not issue an NtO but keep a record of the unpaid penalty charge. Every year the Foreign and Commonwealth Office will request details of all unpaid PCNs and then seek payment from the relevant contraveners.

Charge Certificate

10.48   The Charge Certificate tells the vehicle owner that the penalty charge has been increased and that action will be taken to recover the amount due through the County Court if it is not paid within 14 days. Unless the Secretary of State authorises a departure from the guidelines, the increase in the penalty charge must[110] be set at the applicable surcharge – currently 50 per cent.

10.49   **The authority may issue a Charge Certificate where an NtO has been served** (this includes where a regulation 10 PCN has been served) **the penalty charge has still not been paid and no representation or appeal is under consideration. This must not[111] be done before the end of 28 days beginning with the date on which the NtO was served.**

10.50   Where representations have been made and rejected, and no appeal has been made, the enforcement authority must not[112] issue the Charge Certificate before the end of 28 days beginning with the date on which the Notice of Rejection (NoR) was served. This is to give the vehicle owner time in which to appeal.

10.51   Where cases go to adjudication, authorities must not[113] issue a Charge Certificate before all due processes have been completed. If an appeal is made and withdrawn before the hearing the authority may, after 14 days beginning with the date on which the appeal was withdrawn, issue the Charge Certificate. If an authority issues a Charge Certificate before an appeal is decided, the adjudicator may then cancel the PCN on the grounds of procedural impropriety. The authority should cancel the void Charge Certificate.

10.52   Where an appeal is made but refused, the authority must not issue a Charge Certificate before the end of 28 days beginning with the date on which the adjudicator's decision was served on the appellant.[114]

---

110 S.I. 2007/3487, Schedule, regulation 2(2)
111 S.I. 2007/3483, regulation 21
112 S.I. 2007/3483, regulation 21
113 S.I. 2007/3487, regulation 21, and S.I. 2007/3482, regulation 4(5)(b)
114 S.I. 2007/3483, regulation 21

10.53 If the penalty charge has not been paid 14 days after the Charge Certificate was served, the authority may apply to the Traffic Enforcement Centre at Northampton County Court to recover the increased charge as if it were payable under a county court order.

Registering the Charge Certificate with the Traffic Enforcement Centre

10.54 The Traffic Enforcement Centre (TEC) at Northampton County Court processes requests to register Charge Certificates and requests for authority to enforce orders to recover unpaid parking penalty charges. The TEC's Code of Practice for authorities describes the procedures where a penalty charge has not been paid following service of a Charge Certificate. The Code of Practice is specified within the TEC's rules of membership and is issued to all prospective CPE authorities who register via the TEC their intention to enforce PCNs in accordance with Part 75 of the Civil Procedure Rules.

Witness Statement (formerly a Statutory Declaration)

10.55 Where a Charge Certificate has been served but the penalty charge not paid after 14 days, the authority may apply to the TEC to register the Charge Certificate and recover the increased penalty charge as if it were payable under a County Court order. A fee of £5.00[115] is payable for the registration of each Charge Certificate. The authority must allow 21 days from the date that the Charge Certificate was posted before registering it. Once registered, the TEC will send the enforcement authority a sealed authority to issue an order for the recovery of the amount outstanding – the unpaid penalty charge, any costs awarded against the motorist by an adjudicator, plus the registration fee.

10.56 Within seven days the enforcement authority must then send an order informing the motorist that, within a further 21 days from receipt of the order, s/he must either pay the amount outstanding or send to the TEC a Witness Statement (formerly a Statutory Declaration) to refute the need to pay the penalty charge and that the registration of the unpaid penalty charge should be revoked.

10.57 The Witness Statement can be made on one of the following grounds:[116]

- s/he did not receive the NtO in question;

- s/he made representations to the enforcement authority about the penalty charge and did not receive a rejection;

- s/he appealed to the parking adjudicator against the enforcement authority's decision to reject his/her representation but either received no response to the appeal; the appeal had not been determined by the time that Charge Certificate had been served; or the appeal was determined in his/her favour; or

---

115 As at 01/08/07. Please check the figure on the TEC website www.hmcourts-service.gov.uk
116 S.I. 2007/3483, regulation 23 (2)

- s/he paid in full the penalty charge to which the Charge Certificate relates.

10.58 A valid witness statement automatically revokes the order for the recovery of the unpaid penalty charge and the Charge Certificate. Where the motorist has declared that s/he did not receive the NtO to which the Charge Certificate relates, the NtO is also deemed to have been cancelled. The enforcement authority must therefore address the procedural error specified in the motorist's Witness Statement and decide whether it intends to continue to press for payment of the outstanding penalty charge.

10.59 If the motorist claims that s/he did not receive the NtO it is advisable that the enforcement authority serves a second NtO personally by a process server.

10.60 If the motorist claims that s/he paid the penalty charge or made representations to the enforcement authority about the penalty charge and did not receive a rejection the authority must[117] refer the case to a parking adjudicator who may give such direction as s/he considers appropriate.

10.61 If the motorist claims that s/he appealed to the parking adjudicator against the enforcement authority's decision to reject the representation but received no response to the appeal the enforcement authority must[118] refer the case to a parking adjudicator, who may give such direction as s/he considers appropriate.

10.62 Issuing a Charge Certificate prematurely or, for instance, before a decision about a representation or an appeal has been notified is a procedural irregularity (see Chapter 11). It is one of the grounds on which an adjudicator may now consider an appeal. Authorities should ensure that their systems are not programmed to send out Charge Certificates regardless of circumstances.

10.63 Authorities should note that some of the information above may change following the review of Part 75 of the Civil Procedure Rules.

Warrants of Execution and Certificated Bailiffs

10.64 Where the motorist has been served with an order for recovery of the unpaid penalty charge and fails to pay the penalty charge or to complete the Witness Statement, the authority can ask the TEC for authority to prepare a Warrant of Execution. This authorises a certificated bailiff to seize and sell goods belonging to the motorist to the value of the outstanding amount plus the cost of executing the warrant.

10.65 A local authority can ask the TEC for authority to prepare a Warrant of Execution if **all** of the following criteria are met:

- 21 days have elapsed since service of the registration order was effected;
- full payment has not been received;

---

117 S.I. 2007/3483, regulation 23(7)
118 S.I. 2007/3483, regulation 23(2)(d)

- no Witness Statement has been filed;
- no time extension for making a Witness Statement has been approved; and
- the motorist lives in England or Wales.

10.66 Registration with the TEC can be transferred to the Sheriff's Court in Scotland so that enforcement can be carried out against a motorist whose vehicle is registered at an address in Scotland.[119] However, registration against a motorist whose vehicle is registered at an address in the Isle of Man, the Channel Islands or a foreign country cannot be enforced.

10.67 The authority must produce a warrant within seven days of receipt of the authorisation to do so from the TEC. A copy of the warrant should be given to a certificated bailiff for execution (i.e. a bailiff who holds a general certificate granted by the Lord Chancellor's Department under the Distress for Rent Rules 1988, as opposed to a bailiff employed by the county court). It will be for each local authority to obtain the services of certificated bailiffs, as necessary, either by employing in-house staff or contracting out the work.

10.68 The certificated bailiff will seek to execute the warrant in broadly the same way that a court order would be executed, but with the following differences:

- a modified schedule of fees, charges and expenses is to be used in calculating bailiffs' costs, and new specimen notices are to be used by bailiffs when executing a warrant of execution;[120] and
- other modifications to the statutory provisions concerning the enforcement of civil court judgments and orders are to apply.[121]

10.69 Sections 82 and 83 of the TMA make equivalent provision to section 78 of the RTA 1991. The secondary legislation made under section 78[122], sections 82(5) and 83(4) carry these instruments over, so that they have effect as if made under the 2004 Act. The warrant of execution must be carried by the certificated bailiff when s/he visits a person or premises with a view to enforcing it. S/he must produce it on demand to anyone who has reasonable grounds to see it. However, if the name on the warrant is incorrect, this would suggest that the order for recovery also gave the incorrect name. If so, the order must be re-served before the authority can ask for permission to prepare a warrant.

10.70 Authorities should instruct their bailiffs to liaise with them before taking this action. If the name or address on the county court order Warrant was incorrect the name or address on the Notice to Owner and the Charge

---

119 Order 35 of the County Court Rules 1981 (SI 1981/1687)

120 The Enforcement of Road Traffic Debts (Certificated Bailiffs) regulations 1993 (SI 1993/2072 (L.17))

121 sections 85 to 104 and 125 of the County Courts Act 1984, the County Court (Amendment No. 2) Rules 1993 (SI 1993/2150 (L.24)) and the Enforcement of Road Traffic Debts Order 1993 (SI 1993/2073 (L.18))

122 Enforcement of Road Traffic Debts Order 1993 (S.I.1993/2073 amended by SI 2001/1386) and the Road Traffic Debts (Certified Bailiffs) regulations 1993 (SI 1993/2072 amended by SI 1998/1351 and 2003/1857))

Certificate may also have been incorrect, and neither have been served on the motorist. If the NtO and/or the Charge Certificate were never served the Warrant of Execution should not be served. An NtO (or Charge Certificate) should be served to the name or the address established by the bailiff.

10.71 If the NtO and the Charge Certificate were served, the order should be re-served. A Warrant of Execution has a lifespan of 12 months only and cannot be reissued. If the authority has failed to recover the charge by means of a warrant within this time and wishes to pursue this means of enforcement, it must ask the TEC for authorisation to prepare another warrant.

10.72 A Warrant of Execution is the normal means of collecting unpaid debts. However, there are circumstances in which an authority can use other means to collect the amount owing:

- if an execution against goods has been attempted, but the bailiff has been unable to seize goods because access to the premises was denied, or the goods had already been removed;

- if the value of the goods seized would not meet the outstanding amount, plus the costs of execution;

- if the value of the goods to be seized would not cover the cost of their removal and sale; and

- if an authority has reason to believe that execution against goods will fail to raise the outstanding debt and the costs of execution.

10.73 Other means of recovering the sum owed cannot be used simply because the motorist has ceased to occupy the premises stated in the warrant of execution. The certificated bailiff has authority to levy against the respondent's goods irrespective of address and the bailiff can therefore amend the details of the address on the warrant and seek to enforce the warrant at the motorist's new address.

10.74 The other means of enforcement are:

- an attachment of earnings order – an order deducting money from the motorist's earnings to discharge the amount outstanding;

- a Third Party Debt order – preventing the motorist withdrawing any money from his or her bank or building society account until the outstanding debt is paid and requiring the bank or building society to discharge the debt using money in the motorist's account; and

- a charging order – preventing the motorist selling his or her house or land unless the outstanding debt is paid.

10.75 An authority can also ask the defendant's local County Court to issue an oral examination. An oral examination is a way of finding out about the motorist's income and expenses in order to decide on the most appropriate means of enforcement.

10.76 If it wishes to issue an Order to Obtain Information from a Judgement Debtor or to enforce judgement using one of the methods set out in this chapter, an authority must ask the TEC to transfer the case to the motorist's local County Court.

10.77 A motorist's credit rating will not be affected by enforcement proceedings, as the debts will not be entered in the Register of County Court Judgements, either while the case is at the TEC or on transfer to another County Court for non-warrant enforcement.

10.78 Authorities should note that some of the terminology and information above will change when the *Tribunals, Courts and Enforcement Act 2007* is implemented. 'Warrants of Execution' will be known as 'Warrants of Control', 'Bailiffs' will be known as 'Enforcement Agents', and goods will no longer be 'seized' but 'taken into control'. In addition there will be a new certification process for enforcement agents, issued under the 2007 Act and its underpinning regulations rather than the Distress for Rent Rules.

CHAPTER 11
Challenges, representations and appeals

11.1 The vehicle owner may dispute the issuing of a PCN at three stages:

- Owners may make so-called 'informal challenges' or 'informal representations' (or 'pre NtO letters') **against the PCN before the authority has served an NtO (this does not apply when the PCN is issued by post as the PCN then acts as the NtO);**[123]

- Once an NtO has been served, an owner may make a formal representation against the NtO to the authority; and

- If a formal representation is rejected the owner may appeal against the Notice of Rejection to an independent adjudicator.

11.2 Once a regulation 10 PCN has been served, there are only two stages at which the vehicle owner may dispute it – formal representations (after the PCN, which is also the NtO) has been served and an appeal against a Notice of Rejection.

11.3 It is in the interests of the authority and the vehicle owner to resolve any dispute at the earliest possible stage. Authorities should take account of the CEO's actions in issuing the PCN, but should always give challenges and representations a fresh and impartial consideration.

11.4 An authority has a discretionary power to cancel a PCN at any point throughout the CPE process. It can do this even when an undoubted contravention has occurred if the authority deems it to be appropriate in the circumstances of the case. Under general principles of public law, authorities have a duty to act fairly and proportionately[124] and are encouraged to exercise discretion sensibly and reasonably and with due regard to the public interest.

11.5 Enforcement authorities have a duty[125] not to fetter their discretion, so should ensure that PCNs, NtOs, leaflets and any other advice they give do not mislead the public about what they may consider in the way of representations. They should approach the exercise of discretion objectively and without regard to

---

[123] S.I. 2007/3482, regulation 3(2). The enforcement authority **must** consider representations made at this stage but if it proceeds to serve a Notice to Owner after receiving such representations, then those or other representations can be made in accordance with S.I. 2007/3482, regulation 4

[124] Failure to act in accordance with the general principles of public law may lead to a claim for a decision to be judicially reviewed

[125] *Ibid*

any financial interest in the penalty or decisions that may have been taken at an earlier stage in proceedings. Authorities should formulate (with advice from their legal department) and then publish their policies on the exercise of discretion. They should apply these policies flexibly and judge each case on its merits. An enforcement authority should be ready to depart from its policies if the particular circumstances of the case warrant it.

11.6 **The process of considering challenges, representations and defence of appeals is a legal process that requires officers dealing with these aspects to be trained in the relevant legislation and how to apply it.** It is recommended that they are well versed in the collection, interpretation and consideration of evidence; writing full, clear but concise responses to challenges, enquiries and representations; presenting the authority's case to adjudicators; and relevant government guidance. Recognised training courses, such as those provided by the British Parking Association, will help officers achieve minimum standards.

11.7 Authorities should ensure that their legal departments are involved in establishing a processing system that meets all the requirements of the law. They should also consult them about complex cases.

11.8 Authorities **must**[126] use first class post for all notices. The regulations say 'may' but this means 'must' as authorities may not use second class post. The term 'first class post' does not imply only using the service provided by the Post Office.[127] The Secretary of State recommends first class post for all out-going documents. Authorities should ensure that the date of service of a notice or a Charge Certificate shall, unless the contrary is proved, be taken to have been effected on the second working day after the day of posting.[128]

11.9 It is for the authority to decide the media that may be used to make an informal or a formal representation (for example, writing, e-mail, telephone). Authorities will need to assure themselves that the ways chosen protect social inclusion and allow the person making the representation to make his/her case clearly and coherently and that there is an adequate audit trail to show what was said if the decision is questioned.

Challenges – also known as informal representations

11.10 Statutory representations cannot be made until an NtO has been served but many motorists are likely to write to authorities before then if they do not believe that a PCN is merited. These objections are known as informal representations or challenges. They can be made at any time up to the receipt of the NtO. **It is likely that an enforcement authority will receive informal challenges**

---

[126] S.I. 2007/3483, regulations 3(1)

[127] Postal Services Act 2000, Schedule 8, paragraph 4(1)

[128] S.I. 2007/3483, regulation 3(2).

against PCNs before they issue the NtO** and authorities **must**[129] consider them (the concept of informal challenge **does not apply to PCNs issued by post where the PCN will act as an NtO).** Authorities **are likely to receive these within the 14 day discount period. Enforcement authorities should give proper consideration and respond to these challenges with care and attention, and in a timely manner in order to foster good customer relations, reduce the number of NtOs sent and the number of formal representations to be considered. The Secretary of State suggests that authorities should respond within 14 days. Enforcement authorities should also have suitably trained staff with the appropriate authority to deal with these challenges.**

11.11   There is no legal requirement for informal challenges to be dealt with by the authority's directly employed staff as opposed to the staff of the enforcement contractor, if there is one. But it may help the authority to make it transparent that it deals with challenges fairly and independently if they are considered in-house. If enforcement is carried out by in-house staff, there should be a clear separation at all but the most senior levels between the CEOs and their managers and staff dealing with challenges.

11.12   The consideration should take into account the grounds for making representations and the authority's own guidelines for dealing with extenuating, or mitigating, circumstances. An authority may wish to provide on their website and in Council offices a form on which the motorist can say why s/he thinks that the penalty charge is not merited, with supporting evidence. As with statutory representations, it is vital to ensure that, whatever ways are available to lodge an informal representation, there is an adequate audit trail of the case, showing what decision was taken and why.

11.13   **If the evidence or circumstances (including mitigating circumstances) provide grounds for cancelling the PCN, then the enforcement authority should do so and let the vehicle owner know.** They should refund promptly any money that has already been paid.

11.14   An authority must decide what constitutes 'satisfactory evidence' and it may be beneficial to give a motorist the benefit of the doubt on the first occasion but question the circumstances more closely if there are any subsequent challenges to a different PCN. Authorities should examine with particular care the alleged circumstances of a challenge that appears to be based on guidance from websites or lobby groups. If a number of motorists have parked their vehicles at the same site in the mistaken belief that this is permitted, the authority should consider what can be done to make the restrictions clearer to the public.

11.15   **If the enforcement authority considers that there are no grounds for cancellation, it should tell the vehicle owner and explain its reasons.** They should also make clear that:

---

129 S.I. 2007/3482, regulation 3(2)(b)

- if the penalty charge is not paid they will issue an NtO that enables the vehicle owner to make a formal representation;
- the authority must consider any representations, even where it has previously concluded that the evidence does not merit cancellation of the PCN;
- if the authority rejects the owner's formal representation s/he will be able to appeal to an independent parking adjudicator, who will be able to consider whether the motorist's case falls within any of the statutory grounds for appeal; and
- it is not possible to appeal to a parking adjudicator without going through the process of making a formal representation to the local authority.

11.16 **If a challenge is received within the discount period and subsequently rejected, the Secretary of State recommends that the enforcement authority should consider re-offering the discount for a further 14 days to incentivise payment. Authorities should always make it clear that an owner who has an informal challenge rejected may still make a formal challenge if an NtO is served.**[130]

11.17 If the challenge is received after the 14 day discount period and it is rejected, the authority should consider re-offering the discount if circumstances have adversely affected the ability of the motorist to challenge within 14 days.

Formal representations

11.18 **Many enforcement authorities contract out on-street and car park enforcement and the consideration of informal representations. Enforcement authorities should not contract out the consideration of formal representations. Enforcement authorities remain responsible for the whole process, whether they contract out part of it or not,** and should ensure that a sufficient number of suitably trained and authorised officers are available to decide representations on their merits in a timely and professional manner.

11.19 **Where CPE on-street and car park enforcement and associated operations are done by in-house staff, there should be a clear separation between the staff that decide on the issuing and processing of PCNs and the staff that decide on representations. This is particularly important for cases referred back by the adjudicators. It ensures that decisions are seen to be impartial.**

11.20 Officers dealing with formal representations should be familiar with all aspects of civil parking enforcement, particularly the legal nature of the process, so that they can judge whether or not a representation falls within the statutory grounds[131] or the authority's guidelines for exceptional cases. Fair and efficient systems for carrying out this work should ensure

---

130 S.I. 2007/3482, regulation 3(2)
131 S.I. 2007/3482, regulation 4(4)

that the number of cases going to an adjudicator is minimised – so saving the authority time and expense – without allowing motorists who have committed a contravention to evade the appropriate penalty.

11.21 Elected members may wish to review their parking representations policies, particularly in the area of discretion, to ensure consistency with published policies. However, elected members and unauthorised staff should not, under any circumstances, play a part in deciding the outcome of individual challenges or representations. This is to ensure that only fully trained staff make decisions on the facts presented. The authority's standing orders should be specific as to which officers have the authority to cancel PCNs. There should also be a clear audit trail of decisions taken with reasons for those decisions.

11.22 The grounds on which representations may be made are set out in the regulations[132] and must[133] be stated on the Notice to Owner. Representations must be to either or both of the following effects:

- that, in relation to the alleged contravention on account of which the NtO was served, one or more of the grounds specified below apply; or

- that, whether or not any of those grounds apply, there are compelling reasons why, in the particular circumstances of the case, the enforcement authority should cancel the PCN and refund any sum paid on account of it.

11.23 The grounds are:

- *That the alleged contravention did not occur.*

  This is likely to be the most common ground for representations. It includes cases where a vehicle was allegedly loading or unloading in accordance with a TRO, where a PCN was allegedly issued too early by the CEO, or where a vehicle was allegedly displaying a valid permit, ticket, voucher or badge.

- *That the recipient:*

  - *never was the owner of the vehicle in question;*
  - *had ceased to be its owner before the date on which the alleged contravention occurred; or*
  - *became its owner after that date.*

  Where a recipient makes representations under the second or third circumstances above, he or she is legally obliged to include a statement of the name and address of the person to whom the vehicle was disposed of (or from whom it was acquired, as the case may be), if they have that information.

- *That the vehicle had been permitted to remain at rest in the place in question by a person who was in control of the vehicle without the consent of the owner.*

---

[132] S.I. 2007/3482, regulations 4, 8 and 11
[133] S.I. 2007/3482, regulation 3(3)

This ground for representations covers stolen vehicles, and vehicles which were not stolen but which were used without the owner's consent. It may apply in limited circumstances where a vehicle was being used by a member of the owner's family without the owner's consent, such as where the family member has no permission to use the vehicle and has taken the keys without the owner's knowledge.

- *That the recipient is a vehicle-hire firm[134] and:*
  - *the vehicle in question was at the material time hired from that firm under a vehicle hiring agreement;[135] and*
  - *the person hiring it had signed a statement of liability acknowledging his liability in respect of any PCN served in respect of any contravention involving the vehicle.*

The Secretary of State suggests that the NtO requests that the hire-firm supply to the authority the name and address of the person hiring the vehicle at the material time and a copy of the statement of liability. This information should be used to issue a second NtO on the person hiring the vehicle (who is deemed to be the owner of the vehicle for the purposes of processing the PCN).

- *That the penalty charge exceeded the amount applicable in the circumstances of the case.*

- *That there has been a procedural impropriety on the part of the enforcement authority.*

The regulations define a procedural impropriety as a failure by the enforcement authority to observe any requirement imposed on it by the TMA or the TMA regulations in relation to the imposition or recovery of a penalty charge or other sums. It includes, in particular, the taking of any step, whether or not involving the service of a document and the purported service of a Charge Certificate in advance of the time scale set out in the regulations.[136] This will also be ground for a representation against a PCN that has been served if a fixed penalty notice, as defined by section 52 of the Road Traffic Offenders Act 1988, has been given in respect of that conduct, or the conduct constituting the parking contravention in respect of which the penalty charge notice has been given is the subject of criminal proceedings. This is only likely to be the case on or near pedestrian crossings.

- *That the Order which is alleged to have been contravened in relation to the vehicle concerned is invalid.[137]*

This ground is only available in limited circumstances, because it does not apply to orders to which Part VI of Schedule 9 to the RTRA 1984 applies.

---

134 'vehicle-hire firm' has the same meaning as in section 66 of the Road Traffic Offenders Act 1988

135 'hiring agreement' has the same meaning as in section 66 of the Road Traffic Offenders Act 1988

136 S.I. 2007/3482, regulation 4(5)

137 This does not apply to Orders to which Part VI of Schedule 9 of the Road Traffic regulation Act 1984 applies, as they can only be questioned in proceedings set out in paragraph 35 of Schedule 9

- In the case where a PCN was served by post on the basis that a CEO was prevented by some person from fixing it to the vehicle concerned or handing it to the owner or person in charge of the vehicle, that no CEO was so prevented.

- That the NtO should not have been served because the penalty charge had already been paid in full or by the amount reduced by any discount set[138] within the period set.

11.24 **Authorities must[139] consider representations made on any grounds. Representations must be made within 28 days of service of the NtO. Authorities have the discretion to accept late representations, and we encourage them to use this discretion when a vehicle owner gives a valid reason for the delay and has strong grounds for representations.**

Representations against immobilisation or removal

11.25 The grounds on which representations (and appeals) against the immobilisation or removal of a vehicle can be made differ in some respects to those against the serving of a PCN.[140]

11.26 The grounds against immobilisation are that:

- the vehicle had not been permitted to remain at rest in a CEA in circumstances in which a penalty charge was payable under regulation 4 of S.I. 2007/3483;

- the vehicle had been permitted to remain at rest in the place where it was by a person who was in control of the vehicle without the consent of the owner;

- the place where the vehicle was at rest was not in a CEA;

- in accordance with limitations on the power to immobilise vehicles set out in S.I. 2007/3483, there was in the circumstances of the case no power to immobilise the vehicle at the time at which it was immobilised or at all;

- the penalty charge or other charge paid to secure the release of the vehicle exceeded the amount applicable in the circumstances of the case; or

- there was a procedural impropriety on the part of the enforcement authority.

11.27 The grounds against removal are that:

- the vehicle had not been permitted to remain at rest in a CEA for parking contraventions in circumstances in which a penalty charge was payable under regulation 4 of S.I. 2007/3483;

- a CEO had not, in accordance with regulation 9 of S.I. 2007/3483, fixed a PCN to the vehicle or handed such a notice to the person who appeared to him/her to be in charge of the vehicle, before the vehicle was removed;

---

138 The discount must be in accordance with TMA, Schedule 9
139 S.I. 2007/3482, regulation 5 (2)(b)(ii)
140 S.I. 2007/3482, Parts 3 and 4

- at the time the vehicle was removed, the power to remove the vehicle conferred by regulation 5C of the Removal and Disposal of Vehicle Regulations 1986 was, by virtue of paragraph 3 of that regulation, not exercisable;
- the vehicle had been permitted to remain at rest in the place where it was by a person who was in control of the vehicle without the consent of the owner;
- the place where the vehicle was at rest was not in a CEA for parking contraventions;
- the penalty charge or other charge paid to secure the release of the vehicle exceeded the amount applicable in the circumstances of the case; or
- there was a procedural impropriety on the part of the enforcement authority.

Consideration of representations

11.28 **The enforcement authority must**[141] **consider representations and any supporting evidence against a Notice to Owner,** regulation 10 PCN **or immobilisation or removal, and serve notice of its decision on the person making the representations within 56 days of the service of the representations** whether or not it accepts that the ground in question has been established. **The 56 day period in the regulations should be seen as the maximum period and authorities should aim to decide representations as quickly as possible. The Secretary of State considers that all decision notices should be served within 21 days.**

11.29 If an authority accepts a representation against a Notice to Owner, it must[142] cancel the NtO and inform the person concerned that it has done this. It must **refund any sum already paid.** The PCN should also be cancelled, except where the recipient of the NtO proves s/he was not the owner of the vehicle at the time of the alleged contravention or the owner was a vehicle hire company. **Cancellation** (of an NtO) **does not prevent the authority from serving another NtO for the same contravention to another person.**[143]

11.30 **Where an authority accepts a representation against immobilisation or removal, it must refund any sums paid to release the vehicle, except to the extent (if any) to which those sums were properly paid.**[144] **Where the removed vehicle has already been sold and representations against removal are accepted, the enforcement authority must**[145] **refund all the sale proceeds to the vehicle owner. It is likely that the vehicle owner will already have received the proceeds of the sale minus the cost of removal, storage and sale, and if this is the case the enforcement authority must**[146] **at this point refund the costs of**

---

141 S.I. 2007/3482, regulations 5, 9 and 12
142 S.I. 2007/3482, regulation 5(3)
143 S.I. 2007/3482, regulation 5(4)
144 S.I. 2007/3482, regulation 9(4)
145 RTRA, section 101A (2)
146 RTRA, section 101A(2)

removal, storage and sale. Any authority that undertakes immobilisation or removal should ensure that its staff are fully familiar with the relevant legislation.[147]

11.31 Where a response or notice of decision is likely to be delayed for any reason, the enforcement authority should acknowledge receipt of the representation and explain the representation process, including when a decision notice will be dispatched.

Providing false information

11.32 A person who recklessly or knowingly makes a representation to the authority or an adjudicator which is false in a material particular is guilty of an offence. On summary conviction they may be liable to a fine not exceeding level 5 on the standard scale (currently £5,000).

Notification of the outcome of representations

11.33 Once an authority has come to a decision about a representation, it should promptly tell the person making the representation (usually the owner of the vehicle) what they have decided to do and why. If the person making the representation is not the owner (but is acting officially on their behalf) then the owner should be informed, where possible, of the decision.

11.34 If the authority rejects the representation, it must[148] serve a Notice of Rejection (NoR) stating that it will issue a Charge Certificate unless the PCN is paid, or an appeal made to an adjudicator. The notice of rejection must[149] set out the general form and manner in which an appeal can be made and that the adjudicator has the power to award costs against either party.

11.35 The Notice of Rejection may contain such other information as the local authority considers appropriate. This could include the effect of the Charge Certificate to increase the penalty charge. **The authority should give the owner clear and full reasons for its decision on a representation, in addition to the minimum required information.** This is not just a courtesy to the motorist. Failure to explain such a decision might be seen as maladministration and experience suggests that the provision of relevant information reduces the number of cases taken to adjudication. Moreover, where disputes do go to an adjudicator,

---

[147] The removal and disposal of vehicles by local authorities is governed by sections 99 to 103 of the Road Traffic Regulation Act 1984 and the Removal and Disposal of Vehicles Regulations 1986 (S.I. 1986/183 as amended. See in particular S.I. 2007/3484 which inserts a new regulation 5C into the 1986 regulations whereby civil enforcement officers are authorised to remove illegally parked vehicles from roads in civil enforcement areas). Representations and Appeals against charges for removal, storage and disposal are governed by Part 4 of S.I. 2007/3482 and the setting of those charges by Schedule 9 to the Traffic Management Act 2004 and, outside London, by S.I. 2007/3482

[148] S.I. 2007/3482, regulation 6

[149] S.I. 2007/3482, regulation 6

the local authority's case will rely to quite a large extent on the notice of rejection, so it is in the authority's interest to set out in sufficient detail its reasons for rejecting a motorist's representations. Authorities may wish to attach to the Notice of Rejection a separate form on which the recipient can make his or her appeal.

11.36 **If, following an unsuccessful representation, an authority decides to offer a new discount period for prompt payment, it should set out the dates of this period in the Notice of Rejection.**

Adjudication

11.37 **Adjudicators are appointed jointly by all the relevant local authorities with CPE powers, with the agreement of the Lord Chancellor, and are wholly independent. They have a judicial position and should be treated accordingly.**

11.38 **If a local authority rejects a formal representation, the person who made the representation has the right to appeal to an adjudicator within 28 days of the date of service of the NoR.**[150] **An adjudicator has the discretion in appropriate circumstances to consider an appeal made after 28 days. The grounds for appeal are the same as those for formal representations and are set out in the regulations**[151] (see paragraphs 11.23 to 11.27).

11.39 **If an adjudicator allows the appeal, s/he may** make such **direct**ions to **the authority** s/he considers appropriate, most usually **to cancel the** PCN, the **NtO and refund any sum already paid in respect of the penalty charge. The authority must**[152] **comply with this direction without delay.**

11.40 **The adjudicator's decision is final, subject to the power of adjudicators to review a decision**[153]**. No further challenges can be made other than on a point of law through an application to the High Court for judicial review.**

11.41 **The Government's Tribunals for Users programme emphasises the importance of feedback to improve the representations and appeals procedure and help prevent unnecessary appeals.**

11.42 Persistently losing cases at appeal is time wasting and expensive. It also undermines public confidence in the process that the authority is administering. If an authority is losing a noticeably larger proportion of appeals than comparable authorities, they should consider the possible reasons for this. Consultation with comparable authorities and stakeholders may help to identify factors. There may be simple changes that can be made to ensure that the situation does not continue.

---

150 S.I. 2007/3483, regulation 7
151 S.I. 2007/3483, regulation 13 and Schedule, Paragraphs 7 and 10
152 S.I. 2007/3483, regulation 13 and Schedule, Paragraphs 7 and 10
153 S.I. 2007/3483, Schedule, Paragraph 12

11.43 Authorities should ensure that they have in place a mechanism by which general lessons are learnt from the decisions of adjudicators on their own cases and the cases of other authorities. Those lessons should be built into the practices of the authority and the decisions taken on representations.

Cases referred back to the authority by the adjudicator

11.44 An adjudicator may only allow an appeal if one of the statutory grounds for appeal applies. Where a contravention has taken place but the adjudicator considers that the enforcement authority should have used its discretion to cancel the NtO, the adjudicator may refer the case back for the enforcement authority to reconsider.[154] This power covers appeals against immobilisation or removal as well as against NtOs. **Such cases should be directed to the Office of the Chief Executive** to ensure that the case is given proper consideration on the facts presented without preconceptions. It should not be dealt with by the team who considered the original representation.

11.45 A decision must[155] be reached within 35 days from the notice of the adjudicator's decision. If the enforcement authority does not reach a decision within this period, it is deemed to have accepted the adjudicator's recommendation and must[156] cancel the NtO. The enforcement authority must[157] have regard to the reasons given by the adjudicator for his/her recommendation. Where it does not accept this recommendation it must[158] notify the adjudicator and the appellant of the reasons for its decision before issuing the Charge Certificate.

11.46 If the penalty charge is not paid after 28 days beginning with the date on which the authority notified the appellant that it does not accept the adjudicator's recommendation, the authority may issue a Charge Certificate.

11.47 **If the enforcement authority decides to accept the recommendation of the adjudicator, it must[159] cancel the NtO without delay and refund any sums paid in relation to the NtO.** Refunds in relation to immobilised or removed vehicles **must**[160] be made within 35 days of the adjudicator's direction.

---

154 S.I. 2007/3483, regulations 7(4), 10(5) and 13(5)
155 S.I. 2007/3482, regulations 7(5), 10(6) and 13(6)
156 S.I. 2007/3483, regulation 13(8) and regulation 10(8)
157 S.I. 2007/3483, regulation 13(8) and regulation 10(8)
158 S.I. 2007/3483, regulation 13(7) and regulation 10(7)
159 S.I. 2007/3483, regulation 13(8) and regulation 10(8)
160 S.I. 2007/3483, regulations 10(9) and 13(9)

CHAPTER 12
Key criteria when applying for the power to enforce parking regulations

12.1 The key criteria on which DfT will be need to be satisfied are that:

- the authority has reviewed its existing parking policies and analysed how CPE will contribute to overall transport objectives;
- the authority has consulted as required and taken account of their views in finalising the application;
- proposed penalty charges are proportionate to the scale of the traffic management issues facing the enforcement authority;
- there is consistency with neighbouring schemes so that motorists and others affected can understand how it works; and
- all Traffic Regulation Orders (TROs), traffic signs and road markings are in compliance with legal requirements and the traffic signs and road markings are consonant with the orders.

12.2 Before making an application for CPE designation to the Secretary of State, the authority should consult:

- other traffic authorities (including the Highways Agency) who may be affected;
- the emergency services;
- the DVLA;
- the adjudication service; and
- the Traffic Enforcement Centre at Northampton County Court.

Other powers received along with the power to enforce parking

Immobilisation and removal

12.3 When an authority receives the power to enforce parking it will also receive the power to immobilise or remove vehicles parked in contravention. The Secretary of State does not expect authorities to use the immobilisation power except for persistent evaders. But s/he accepts that authorities may have to remove vehicles in order to keep traffic moving.

Bus lanes

12.4 When an authority applies to the Secretary of State for the power to enforce parking under part 6 of the Traffic Management Act 2004 the Secretary of State expects them also to apply for the power to enforce bus lanes under the Transport Act 2000. The Secretary of State currently intends that once the provisions in Part 6 of the TMA covering bus lanes are in place, the same procedure will apply. The provisions with respect to certain moving traffic matters may be different. The Secretary of State recommends that an authority new to civil enforcement familiarise itself with the concepts by enforcing parking before undertaking the enforcement of bus lanes and certain moving traffic contraventions.

Special Enforcement Areas (SEAs)

12.5 The TMA enables authorities with CPE power to enforce in a Special Enforcement Area (SEA)[161] prohibitions of double parking[162] and parking at dropped footways[163] as if they had been introduced using a Traffic Regulation Order (Traffic Management Order in London). An SEA must be within a CEA or cover the same area as one. An authority should consider whether to apply for SEA designation as part of their CEA application. If they do, they will have to apply under Schedule 10 paragraph 3 (1) – (4) asking the Secretary of State to designate the relevant part of their area as an SEA.

Authorities eligible to apply for CPE power

12.6 The authorities eligible to apply for designation orders are county councils, metropolitan district councils (either singly or jointly), unitary authorities and the Council of the Isles of Scilly (that is, the traffic authorities for local roads).

12.7 Metropolitan district councils should apply for orders covering the whole of their area (or their areas, in the case of joint applications). County councils and the Council of the Isles of Scilly may apply for orders covering all or part of their area. Where a county council is considering civil enforcement, it is preferable if the application includes all the boroughs and districts with a single commencement date. However, if this is not possible the DfT is prepared to consider staggered applications, but no more than three tranches within a county area. District, borough, unitary and metropolitan district councils should apply for orders covering the whole of their administrative area. The Order will not cover military roads in the CPE area.

12.8 The Secretary of State will not be able to prioritise a request for small changes to the area covered by an existing CEA, so authorities should carefully consider the area to be included in the original designation.

---

161 TMA, Schedule 10
162 TMA, section 85
163 TMA, section 86

Co-operation between district councils and county councils

12.9 Non-metropolitan district councils in England will not be able to apply for designation orders. It is important that there should be very close co-operation between districts and their county. The district might lead in preparing an application and, under an agency agreement, carrying out enforcement on behalf of the county.

12.10 The civil enforcement of off-street parking restrictions within CEAs reinforces the need for co-operation. The Secretary of State is aware that in most areas with two tiers of local government it is the district councils that own and operate most local authority off-street car parks. Where these districts also act as agent for their county, there should be significant efficiency gains in having a unified civil parking enforcement operation.

12.11 In some cases the county council carries out on-street parking enforcement directly and districts enforce off-street parking. This approach seems likely to be less efficient than having one enforcing authority. County councils may wish to consider allowing their districts to carry out on-street enforcement under agency agreements.

12.12 The county council would need to indicate in their application if it proposed to exclude some or all off-street car parks from the designation order and use the RTRA 1984 for off-street enforcement. The Secretary of State will only consider allowing this in very exceptional circumstances. This is to make the new arrangements easier for the public to understand. It also helps make parking enforcement cost-effective by unifying restricted, permitted and off-street operations in the same area. The Secretary of State recommends that a CPE application is delayed if a district or borough is not prepared to include its off-street car parking within a CEA.

12.13 District councils in England that would like responsibility for parking enforcement should approach their county council as soon as possible to check that the county would be willing to apply for orders in respect of the district. All district councils will need to check that their county council would enter into an agency agreement enabling the district council to use the powers.

Consulting other local authorities

12.14 The Secretary of State expects local authorities to consult neighbouring authorities before applying for designation orders. The consultation should cover the proposed levels of penalty charges. It should also cover opportunities for co-operation, in the form of shared facilities or services, immediately or in the longer term. If a county council applies in respect of one or more of its districts, it should consult the adjacent district councils within the county, as well as any adjacent authorities outside the county likely to be affected or with which it might want to co-operate.

12.15 It is recommended that the authority explain its proposals to representatives of any parish, town or community councils in its area.

12.16 Consultation is particularly important where authorities share a common built-up area or there are heavy traffic flows across the boundaries.

12.17 Authorities should consider the following:

- improved enforcement by one authority, but not by its neighbour, can transfer a parking problem from one authority to another;

- where possible, neighbouring authorities should use parking charges and parking penalty charges that are similar, to ensure consistency for road users;

- the public should be clear about which authority is responsible for parking policy and for parking enforcement. The Traffic Signs Regulations 2002 allow the name of the traffic authority to appear on parking place signs but where the enforcement authority is not the traffic authority, DfT would have to give special authorisation to include the name of the district or borough council on signs; and

- neighbouring CPZs should harmonise their hours of operation to reduce confusion, although this may not be practical if parking demand patterns vary significantly in adjoining areas, or where short duration controls are used to deter commuter parking. The extent and duration of CPZ controls should be clear to the public.

Consulting other bodies

12.18 Authorities applying for CPE powers need to make an agreement with DVLA about information provision. They should approach DVLA about this before making their fornal application. See paragraphs 10.37 to 10.42 above.

The continuing role of the police

12.19 When an authority receives CPE power the police service is specifically excluded from yellow line parking enforcement. But the police retain sole responsibility for certain non-yellow line parking offences in a civil enforcement area:

- enforcing certain non-yellow line parking offences, principally endorsable offences such as dangerous parking, obstruction, and failure to comply with police 'no parking' signs placed in emergencies;

- enforcing the full range of moving traffic offences and infringements;

- acting against any vehicle where security or other traffic policing issues are involved, including the need to close roads or set up diversions; and

- enforcing all parking restrictions on roads outside CEAs.

12.20 The TMA gives authorities the power, among other things, to enforce prohibitions on vehicles stopping on or near pedestrian crossings.[164] This is the only area subject to civil parking enforcement where the police have retained the power of enforcement.[165] If the enforcement authority and the police both take enforcement action, the criminal action takes precedence and the PCN must be cancelled. If the PCN has been paid, the money **must**[166] be refunded.

12.21 The Secretary of State is under a statutory duty to consult the appropriate chief officer of police before making any designation orders to create CEAs. Local authorities should discuss their proposals to introduce civil parking enforcement with the police at an early stage and act on the advice of the police. Matters discussed should include the proposed timetable and geographic boundaries and whether the enforcement regime will include immobilisation and/or removals. Consultation should specify a plan for a smooth and orderly transfer of responsibilities.

---

164 TMA – Schedule 7 paragraphs 3 (2)(c) and (h)(i), and 4(2)(c) and (i)(i)

165 S.I. 2007/3483, regulation 7

166 S.I. 2007/3483, regulation 7

CHAPTER 13
What an authority should do before taking on parking enforcement power

Formulating and appraising parking policies

13.1 Before applying to the Secretary of State for orders creating CEAs, a local authority should appraise its parking policies and the way those policies are being implemented, to see which traffic management objectives are being met and where improvements are needed. Unless the authority has regularly appraised its parking policies, this can be a major task. The authority needs to allow sufficient time and resources for the results to be of value.

13.2 If an authority has not already done so, it should develop parking policies that are consistent with and contribute to their overall transport policy. These should have particular regard to the provisions in Chapters 2 and 3.

13.3 Where an authority has already formulated its parking policies, it should appraise these, taking account of Chapter 4. This review should cover the matters set out in Chapter 4.

13.4 The Secretary of State strongly recommends that the public should have easy access to an authority's parking policies, including its enforcement policies and priorities. This makes the authority more accountable and should also help it to counter accusations that enforcement is being carried out arbitrarily or unfairly.

13.5 If the authority does not already monitor the effectiveness of its parking policies, it should put in place procedures for doing so as early as possible before introducing CPE, so they can judge its impact on road safety and congestion.

Traffic Regulation Orders (TROs)

13.6 The appraisal of parking policy should include the scope and relevance of all existing on-street and off-street TROs. It should include how they need to change to meet the authority's parking policy objectives. The review of the TROs should check whether the restrictions indicated by traffic signs and road markings are the same as those authorised by the TRO and make them consistent if they are not. The Secretary of State **will not** sign an Order until a senior official of the authority has confirmed in writing that all existing and new TROs, traffic signs and road markings in the proposed CEA:

- have been reviewed;
- are in line with Government regulations[167] and guidance in relevant chapters of the *Traffic Signs Manual* or have special authorisation from DfT;
- are consistent with each other; and
- are in a good state of repair.

13.7 It is recommended that this confirmation is based on an independent audit by a qualified consultant. An adjudicator may uphold appeals against PCNs issued where parking controls are not properly indicated with traffic signs and/or road markings. Annex E gives advice on appraising the adequacy of traffic signs, plating and road markings and Annex F on appraising TROs.

13.8 The authority will need to consider whether TRO restrictions should apply beyond the normal working day and/or at weekends. The authority should examine the scope for relaxing or removing any redundant parking controls. Unnecessary restrictions are very quickly identified when the authority takes over responsibility for their enforcement and this can result in complaints from motorists and bad publicity. It is better to deal with them before starting civil enforcement.

13.9 Local authorities may also wish to consider placing all their TROs on a geographical information system and on their website, so that they can supply their contractors with accurate, up-to-date maps, and the public can find out where and when parking is permitted and not permitted.

13.10 As part of their appraisal of TROs, authorities should identify the technical changes needed to comply with the Traffic Management Act 2004. For example, amendments will be needed to reflect the switch from traffic offence provisions to the new system of penalty charges and civil liabilities. Existing on-street and off-street parking orders will need to be amended to reflect the removal of 'initial' and 'excess' parking periods. Ideally this changeover should be when CPE comes into force. If this is not possible, authorities may include a provision, valid for no more than three months from the introduction of CPE, so that CEOs can serve a penalty charge when the excess charge flag or display is showing. They may need to make similar provision in off-street car park orders where parking meters are used. This will give them time to replace obsolete 'excess charge' indicators on parking meters.

13.11 The authority may wish to retain in their TROs a provision relating to anything done with the permission or at the direction of a police constable in uniform to cover emergency situations.

---

167 Principally the Traffic Signs Regulations and General Directions 2002 (S.I. 2002/3113) or subsequent editions substituted

13.12 Once an authority has CPE, their TROs should not cover the means of enforcement or the level of penalty charges. National legislation covers these.

Pavement parking

13.13 Parking a heavy goods vehicle (HGV) on the footway contravenes section 19 of the Road Traffic Act 1988 and can be enforced by a Civil Enforcement Officer in a CEA. Pavement parking by all motorised vehicles is banned throughout London (except where expressly permitted) and in some other parts of England by local Acts of Parliament. In these circumstances the ban does not need to be signed but compliance may be better if it is. Any authority may introduce a ban on pavement parking in a CEA with a TRO and their CEOs may enforce it. Such a ban **must** be indicated with traffic signs authorised by DfT.[168] Physical measures such as high kerbs and bollards will increase compliance.

13.14 During the appraisal of their parking policies, an authority should consider whether pavement parking is a problem in any part of its area. If it is, and it is not covered by an existing TRO, the authority may wish to consider amending their TROs, or making new ones.[169]

13.15 The Secretary of State recommends that if an authority wants to prohibit pavement parking, it publicises the provisions of the ban, the reasons for it and the date of introduction.

Choosing the most appropriate package of enforcement measures

13.16 Once an authority has appraised its parking policies, capacity, controls, usage and enforcement, it should decide whether it needs to adjust the policies and what changes, if any, it needs to make to achieve its objectives. In particular, it will need to consider what type of enforcement regime would achieve an acceptable level of compliance. The type of enforcement regime available to local authorities can be varied according to local circumstances. It is important that authorities consider the factors in paragraphs 13.17 to 13.23 below.

Enforcement on trunk roads and other high speed roads

13.17 It has, in the past, been considered inappropriate for local authorities to use their enforcement powers on high speed roads (including trunk roads) because of the dangers to CEOs. However, the power given in the TMA to use approved devices, which are best suited for use in situations such as on high

---

[168] Copies of working drawings NP 428.1 and 428.2 can be obtained on request from traffic.signs@dft.gsi.gov.uk

[169] sections 2(3), 6(3)(a) and 126 of the RTRA 1984 give the power to make a TRO in respect of any part of the width of a road.

speed roads where stopping and parking are banned, makes local authority enforcement of parking on these roads more practical. Some authorities may now wish to include some high speed roads in their designation orders.

13.18 TMA does not preclude an authority from enforcing parking on a trunk road within a CEA just because its traffic authority is the Secretary of State. If the police and the Highways Agency agree, such applications will be considered because it may be sensible for parking on the trunk road and on surrounding roads to be subject to civil enforcement. If such enforcement by an authority is not feasible or desirable the trunk road would be excluded from the Order and enforcement would continue to be carried out by the police service. The authority would need to agree this with the police and the Highways Agency before submitting the CPE application.

13.19 When a local authority is considering applying to the Secretary of State for orders creating a CEA, the appropriate regional office of the Highways Agency should always be consulted at an early stage.

Level of enforcement

13.20 The level of enforcement required may not be the same throughout the proposed CPE area. To minimise accusations of favouritism, the relative levels of enforcement throughout the CEA should be based clearly on the authority's policy objectives as well as the extent and nature of the parking problems. For example, an authority may decide to target roads where parking problems frequently occur to improve traffic flow, or to target footway parking where this is prohibited to improve the amenity of pedestrians.

Exemptions, waivers and dispensations

13.21 When preparing its application for the Orders creating a CEA, a local authority should consider its policies on parking exemptions, waivers and dispensations for special categories of vehicle user, or vehicle users in special circumstances. These are described in Chapter 9. In some cases, exemptions are statutory and the local authority must honour them. But in other cases there is some scope for authorities to adopt policies to suit local circumstances.

Assessment of the chosen enforcement package

13.22 Once the authority has chosen the most suitable enforcement package, it should assess it against the authority's parking policy objectives. The assessment should cover both the proposed enforcement package itself and any complementary changes (for example, to TROs or to off-street parking charges). The assessment needs to consider:

- whether the enforcement package and associated changes will achieve a level of compliance with parking controls which the authority finds acceptable;
- where motorists who previously offended will park in future;
- whether parking problems in one area will be displaced to another;

- whether the enforcement package and its consequences will be acceptable to the public, and, in particular, to motorists, local businesses and residents;
- what the effects will be on users of public transport, pedestrians and cyclists;
- whether there is adequate provision for special categories of driver, such as disabled people, 'professional carers', drivers delivering or collecting goods, or drivers of statutory undertakers' vehicles (see Chapters 3 and 9); and
- the expected financial results (see Chapters 3 and 14).

13.23 The enforcement package should be adapted to tackle any weaknesses that the assessment reveals.

CHAPTER 14
Financial assessment

14.1 When preparing its application for Orders creating CEAs, a local authority should complete a thorough assessment of the expected costs of and revenues from all aspects of on-street and off-street parking operations. They should draw on in-house or outside expertise, as necessary. The assessment should consider both direct and indirect financial implications. For example, it is unlikely that income from PCNs will cover all new costs, but effective enforcement should result in an increase in income from paid on-street and off-street parking. Authorities should carry out the financial assessment in conjunction with the policy assessment described in Chapters 12 and 13.

14.2 An authority should assess costs, taking account of both start-up costs and running costs once civil parking enforcement is under way. As with all types of financial assessment, it is important that the estimated figures are as realistic as possible.

14.3 Enforcement costs will vary greatly from authority to authority, according to local circumstances. Authorities considering taking on the power to enforce parking should consult authorities who have already done so and the British Parking Association for up-to-date information on likely costs and benefits.

Income – this should include existing income sources, such as off-street car parks, on-street (for example pay-and-display and meter parking, and residents' parking permits), off-street parking operated by the authority on privately owned land,[170] as well as any new income from enforcement. Most local authorities will already have figures for on-street and off-street parking income and will only need to consider the impact that effective enforcement will have on the demand for paid parking. Authorities should note that **all** income from penalty charges is subject to the restrictions on usage in section 55 of the RTRA. Income from immobilisation and vehicle removal, storage and disposal activities should be assessed separately, as these activities should not make a surplus.

Expenditure – this should include all expenditure on in-house staff, contractors (if any), installation, renewal and maintenance of equipment, signs and lines on the highway, and equipment to issue and record parking charges and penalty charges. Even if an authority contracts out enforcement work, it will need to employ back office staff. Authorities should not forget the relevant time that will be required of staff in their legal and Chief Executive's departments to

---

[170] CPE can only apply to privately owned car parks that are regulated by an order made under the Road Traffic Regulation Act 1984, section 35 and provided under any letting or arrangements made by a local authority with some other person (such as a privately-owned company) under Section 33(4) of that Act.

successfully implement CPE. In-house staff costs should include overheads as well as salaries. Authorities should only include the proportion of staff time spent on parking matters.

Client management, publicity and policy review – the cost of these activities will depend to some extent on the enforcement package chosen by the authority and how many functions (if any) are contracted out. However, the authority will always remain responsible for monitoring the effectiveness of civil parking enforcement, and it will need to ensure that sufficient resources are devoted to maintaining and improving quality of service and value for money.

Civil Enforcement Officers – the cost of providing a CEO will vary with geographical location. Authorities should consult the British Parking Association and authorities similar to themselves with CPE powers to get an idea of likely costs. Authorities that already employ staff to issue Excess Charge Notices will have a good idea of costs in their area. These authorities are likely to find that their existing workforce is well placed to carry out CPE enforcement.

PCN processing – this activity can be contracted out or undertaken in-house. If undertaken in-house, authorities may need to invest in new IT equipment.

Immobilisation and removals – fees are set by the Secretary of State or the Mayor of London (see Chapters 8 and 14) based on likely costs. These operations should not generate revenue and so do not affect the financial performance of an authority's enforcement regime.

Dealing with representations – authorities should not contract out the responsibility of dealing with formal representations against PCNs. This is a quasi-legal task and should, where necessary, involve input from the legal department and the Chief Executive's department. It is impossible to estimate the number of representations an authority might receive, but the more accurate the on-street performance, the fewer there are likely to be.

Cases going to adjudication – this is another area where authorities need to ensure that there is adequate input from the legal department and the Chief Executive's department. On average, less than 1 per cent of all PCNs issued have gone to adjudication but it is higher in some authorities. Authorities should ensure that their cost estimates include the annual payments that will need to be made to the adjudication service as well as the staff and legal costs involved in responding to an appeal. Authorities should not think that the way in which the adjudication service is funded makes it cheaper to let a case go to appeal than deal properly with a representation.

Contract management – if any of the tasks are contracted out, the authority will need to devote enough in-house time to ensure that contractual duties and service level agreement (SLA) terms are met.

Training – authorities should take into account the training that will be required before CPE is introduced and afterwards for continuing professional development.

Other costs – the assessment should include the initial costs of reviewing all relevant TROs, signs and lines and putting them into a good state of repair, as well as installing any new signing, plating and road markings required for parking enforcement purposes. If the authority uses in-house enforcement, the assessment will need to take account of the cost of their uniforms and equipment. The assessment also needs to include the costs of replacing and maintaining uniforms and equipment and of collecting cash from parking meters or pay-and-display machines.

14.4 Any income from and expenditure on enforcement by the authority on other land in their ownership such as housing estates should not be included unless they are included in the designation order.

Parking charges

14.5 The setting of charges for parking on-street or off-street in designated areas is a matter for the authority in accordance with the provisions of the Road Traffic Regulation Act 1984. Authorities should review charges periodically and take account of their effectiveness in meeting policy objectives and the criteria in the above paragraphs.

14.6 Local authorities can vary their parking charges using a simplified procedure of public notices under the Local Authorities' Traffic Orders (Procedure) (England and Wales) Regulations 1996. The Secretary of State recommends that authorities set charges at levels which are consistent with the aims of the authority's transport strategy, including its road safety and traffic management strategies.

14.7 Authorities should never use parking charges just to raise revenue or as a local tax. However, where the demand for parking is high, the delivery of transport objectives with realistic demand management prices for parking may result in surplus income. In such cases local authorities **must**[171] ensure that any on-street revenue not used for enforcement is used for legitimate purposes only and that its main use is to improve, by whatever means, transport provision in the area so that road users benefit. The authority's auditor may decline to certify the accounts of a local authority that has used on-street parking income (and all enforcement income) in a way that is not in accordance with the provisions of section 55 of the RTRA.

14.8 When setting charges, authorities should consider the following factors:

- parking charges can help to curb unnecessary car use where there is adequate public transport or walking or cycling are realistic alternatives, for example, in town centres;

---

171 RTRA, section 55

- charges can reflect the value of kerb-space, encouraging all but short-term parking to take place in nearby off-street car parks where available. This implies a hierarchy of charges within a local authority area, so that charges at a prime parking space in a busy town centre would normally be higher than those either at nearby off-street car parks or at designated places in more distant residential areas. Such hierarchies should be as simple as practicable and applied consistently so that charge levels are readily understandable and acceptable to both regular and occasional users;

- charges should be set at levels that encourage compliance with parking restrictions. If charges are set too high they could encourage drivers to risk non-compliance or to park in unsuitable areas, possibly in contravention of parking restrictions. In certain cases they could encourage motorists to park in a neighbouring local authority area which may not have the capacity to handle the extra vehicles. In commercial districts this may have a negative impact on business in the area; and

- if on-street charges are set too low, they could attract higher levels of traffic than are desirable. They could discourage the use of off-street car parks and cause the demand for parking spaces to exceed supply, so that drivers have to spend longer finding a vacant space.

14.9 Local authorities need to decide on a desirable occupancy rate for paid on-street parking spaces. High occupancy rates may in the long term encourage the use of alternative forms of transport (if available) or diversion to another destination. But they may increase congestion in the short term as vehicles search for available spaces. Lower occupancy rates may result in a less efficient use of the limited kerb space available.

14.10 The Secretary of State has received complaints from utility companies about the substantial variation in the charges made by authorities for suspending parking places. Authorities should ensure that these charges are realistic and their basis can be explained to the utility company.

Penalty charges

14.11 Authorities should read Chapter 8 and decide which band of penalty charge to use.

14.12 **The primary purpose of penalty charges is to encourage compliance with parking restrictions. In pursuit of this, enforcement authorities should adopt the lowest charge level consistent with a high level of public acceptability and compliance. The enforcement authority must[172] ensure that the public knows what charge levels have been set by publishing them well in advance of their introduction. They must also publish any subsequent change to the charge levels.[173] In London, charges will be set by the London local authorities acting jointly and by Transport for London (in respect of GLA**

---

172 TMA, Schedule 9 paragraphs 5 (Greater London) and 9 (outside Greater London)
173 *Ibid*

roads), with the approval of the Mayor (and provided that the Secretary of State does not object). Outside London, the charges must accord with guidelines set by the Secretary of State.[174]

14.13 Local authorities outside London may choose between one of two bands of penalty charge. In London there are three bands. Authorities should chose the lowest band that will help achieve a high degree of compliance with the parking regulations while meeting the objective of producing a system of civil parking enforcement that is self-financing. It should be readily accepted and understood by regular and occasional users. This will encourage payment and minimise the cost of recovering unpaid penalty charges.

14.14 In London the levels of penalty charges may be changed by the London local authorities or, as appropriate, Transport for London, subject to the approval of the Mayor of London and no objection to the changes being expressed by the Secretary of State. You can find up-to-date figures on the levels of penalty charges in London on the London Councils website in the 'Parking Enforcement Explained' section.

14.15 The Secretary of State considers that a variety of penalty charge bands, either between authorities or within an individual authority's area, would not be appropriate. In most cases, it will be more effective to tailor an authority's level of enforcement according to the seriousness of non-compliance with parking controls. For example, they may introduce more frequent patrols, immobilisation or removals, rather than to use variable levels of penalty charges. In general, therefore, the Secretary of State would expect a uniform band of penalty charges throughout an authority's area. Where there is more than one penalty charge band within an authority's area it is important that the reason for the variation can be easily understood and accepted by motorists. Variations which appear to be arbitrary (for example along the centre line of a road) may attract criticism.

Discounts and increases to penalty charges

14.16 To encourage prompt payment, the regulations provide[175] for the motorist to receive a discount if the penalty charge is paid within 14 days of the service of the PCN. The discount is currently 50 per cent. Because the motorist does not have the benefit of an informal as well as a formal challenge period, the discount period is 21 days for PCNs sent by post on the basis of evidence from an approved device. Collection costs and the number of representations and appeals to the parking adjudicator can be cut if authorities send prompt and considered replies to informal challenges received within the discount period and offer a further 14 days to pay at the discounted rate if the authority rejects their informal representation. If the penalty is unpaid and no successful representation or appeal is made within the framework and timescales of the statutory process, regulations provide for the penalty charge to increase – currently by 50 per cent.

---

174 S.I. 2007/3487 (for outside London) and section 284 of the Greater London Authority Act 1999 (for inside London)

175 S.I. 2007/3487, Schedule

Table 14.1: PCN amounts outside London payable according to the time within which it is paid

Level of PCN	Paid within 14 days	Paid between 15 days and service of a Notice to Owner	Paid between issue of Notice to Owner and service of Charge Certificate	Paid after service of Charge Certificate
PCN £40	£20	£40	£40	£60
PCN £60	£30	£60	£60	£90

PCN £50	£25	£50	£50	£75
PCN £70	£35	£70	£70	£105

Estimating income from penalty charges

14.17 When assessing likely income from penalty charges (not including immobilisation or removal fees) for their CPE application, authorities will need to estimate the proportion of PCNs that will be:

- at the higher and lower level;
- paid within the discount period;
- paid in full;
- paid after the charge certificate is served; and
- cancelled or go to adjudication.

14.18 There is currently no information to guide authorities on the proportion of PCNs that are likely to be at the higher and lower levels.

14.19 Authorities need to bear in mind that about 50 per cent to 55 per cent of PCNs are paid at the discount rate and 12 per cent are paid at the full rate. The remainder incur additional costs for the authority either from action to pursue payment or to deal with representations and appeals.

Charges and income from vehicle immobilisation, removal, storage and disposal

14.20 Where an authority has to immobilise or remove a vehicle outside London, the charges must accord with guidelines set by the Secretary of State.[176] In London, the charges will be set by the London local authorities acting jointly, with the approval of the Mayor (and provided

---

176 S.I. 2007/3487

Financial assessment – March 2008

the Secretary of State does not object). The charges should be set no higher than required to meet the reasonable costs of the immobilisation/removals procedure. They should not generate a surplus.

Table 14.2 Charges set for vehicle immobilisation, removal, storage and disposal outside London[177]

Type of charge	Amount of charge
Vehicle immobilisation	£40
Vehicle removal	£105
Vehicle storage	£12 for each day, or part of day, during which the vehicle is impounded
Vehicle disposal	£50

Table 14.3: Charges in London

Type of charge	Level of charge[177]
Vehicle immobilisation	£70
Vehicle removal	£200
Vehicle storage	£40 a day
Vehicle disposal	£70

14.21 Authorities should not apply storage charges for removed vehicles until midnight on the day following removal, because it is a harsh additional penalty for motorists who recover their vehicles relatively quickly.

Publication of the level of penalty and other charges

14.22 The level of penalty charges and, where applicable, charges relating to vehicle immobilisation or removal should be properly publicised before civil parking enforcement is introduced and whenever they are changed. Before the CEA designation order is made, the Secretary of State requires an authority to publish in at least one local newspaper notice of the charges it plans to impose. Such notices need to be published at least 14 days before the charges are due to come into force. A list of intended charges will also need to be placed on deposit at council offices in the area concerned.

14.23 Authorities should note that this is a **minimum** legal requirement. They should consider other means of publicity to ensure that motorists are made aware of the levels of penalty and other charges. One option is that shortly before or following the introduction of enforcement, the authority should issue warning notices rather than PCNs to vehicles that are in contravention of restrictions.

---

177 as at 31 March 2008

178 as at 1 July 2007

Changes to penalty and other charges

14.24 Local authorities outside London must choose between the £60/40 band and £70/50 band of penalty charges. Any subsequent change to the charge band must accord with guidelines given by the Secretary of State and be publicised as set out above. Any departure from the Guidelines requires the Secretary of State's permission.[179]

VAT and penalty charge income

14.25 HM Revenue and Customs advise that penalty charges fall outside the scope of VAT, whether the PCN is issued for a contravention on-street or off-street.

---

179 TMAt, Schedule 9 paragraph 8(3)

CHAPTER 15
Application for a CEA designation order

15.1 If an authority wishes to introduce civil parking enforcement in all or part of its area, it must apply to the Secretary of State for one or more appropriate designation orders on the form at the end of this chapter. Chapter 12 describes the authorities that are eligible to apply, and the types of order they may apply for. If the Secretary of State is satisfied with an authority's application, s/he will make an order, or orders, that, if approved by Parliament, would enable the relevant contraventions to be enforced by the authority rather than the police service – either throughout the authority's area, or in a specified part or parts of it.

15.2 It is essential that authorities keep the Department for Transport informed of their plans from the time they decide they would like to apply for these powers. Such liaison should identify and tackle problems at an early stage, so that applications can be processed without delay. If the authority gives DfT no prior warning of an application, there may be delays in processing it.

15.3 Local authorities in England should send their correspondence and applications to:

Traffic Management Division
Department for Transport
Zone 2/06
Great Minster House
76 Marsham Street
London
SW1P 4DR

15.4 They may also e-mail them to Parking.queries@dft.gsi.gov.uk

15.5 Authorities considering applying for CPE power should first contact officials in DfT's Traffic Management Division[180] to discuss the proposed commencement date and any issues relating to the content of the application form (below). The Secretary of State recommends that a county council obtains the agreement of the relevant district/borough council(s) to the introduction of civil parking enforcement before submitting the application. The authority will also need to provide evidence in the formal application that it has consulted with neighbouring traffic authorities, the police, Highways Agency, TEC, DVLA, and the Adjudication service.

---

180 Write to Traffic Management Division branch 1, Zone 2/06 Great Minster House, London SW1P 4DR or ring 020 7944 6483, 020 7944 2484 or 020 7944 3155.

15.6 Authorities should include in their formal application a clear and accurate definition in plain English of the roads that will be excluded from the CEA/SEA. If a county council is applying on behalf of all of its districts, or for more than one district, a list of all the districts should be listed on the front cover of the formal application. The legal names of the county council and all of the district councils should be provided in the application.

15.7 The Secretary of State will consider each application and is under a statutory duty[181] to consult the appropriate chief officer of police before deciding whether to make the requested designation order. S/he also consults the Council for Tribunals and the Highways Agency. The Secretary of State will not consider the application unless all the authorities covered by it are in agreement. Authorities should be prepared to answer questions about their application and provide additional information.

15.8 Once the application has been made the local authority will need to make the necessary minor amendments to its existing TROs so that they can be enforced from the proposed commencement date (see Chapter 13). However, authorities are strongly advised to review their TROs, road signs, lines and markings at least 12 months prior to the proposed commencement date. regulation 21 of The Local Authorities' Traffic Orders (Procedure) (England and Wales) Regulations 1996 provide a simplified and streamlined procedure for consolidation and minor orders. Substantive changes to TROs will take longer to make and procedures for any changes that need to come into force on the commencement of civil parking enforcement will need to be initiated at a suitably early date. Annex F gives further guidance.

15.9 The Secretary of State will not submit the designation order to Parliament for approval unless s/he has received six weeks before its commencement date an undertaking signed by a senior council official confirming that all TROs, traffic signs and road markings in the proposed CEA/SEA have been reviewed and are now lawful, consistent and in good order. Details of the confirmation required is set out in the form at the end of this Chapter. The designation order will then be made and laid before Parliament at least 21 days before it is due to come into force.

15.10 When the Secretary of State is satisfied with the information from the applicant authority and has completed consultations, s/he will signal whether the application is acceptable in principle and s/he is minded to make an appropriate order, subject to the satisfactory completion of outstanding tasks by the authority. The Secretary of State will aim to give his/her agreement within 20 weeks of receiving a formal application.

15.11 Publicity and notice of the proposed level of penalty charges need to have been completed at least 14 days before the commencement date.

---

[181] TMA, Schedule 8 paragraph 2(3)

Table 15.1 Twelve-step application procedure for Civil Parking Enforcement (CPE) powers

The following 12 steps outline the processes that must be completed before Parliament grants an authority decriminalised parking enforcement (CPE) powers.

Step	
1) Initial contact	
a) The local authority notifies the Department of an impending application and the proposed CPE commencement date.	
2) Troubleshooting	
a) At this stage the local authority may seek advice on any issues or if appropriate seek to arrange a meeting/video conference with the Department to discuss these issues in more depth.	
3) Application submission	20 weeks prior to commencement date
a) The local authority submits their formal application in electronic format or 6 hard copies in post.	
4) Application processing	
a) The Department processes the application and responds to the local authority with any comments.	
b) The local authority addresses concerns raised by the Department.	
5) Legal order drafting	
a) The Department drafts a legal order for the requested powers.	
6) Application and legal order consultation	
a) The Department asks for comments from consultees on both the application and draft legal order.	
b) The Department informs the local authority of any issues that need to be resolved as a result of any comments on the application/legal order and asks for any issues to be resolved.	
7) Legal order checking	
a) The Department runs a second legal check on the draft order.	
b) The TRO Confirmation statement will be required at this stage.	
8) Order signing	6 weeks prior to commencement date
a) The Department submits the legal order to the Secretary of State for signing.	
9) Proofing, printing and arrangements for laying of the legal order	
a) The Department sends the legal documents for proofing and printing and arranges for the laying of the order.	
10) Laying of the order before Parliament	At least 21 days (including weekends)

Step	
11) MPs/Council Leader/Determination letters	
a) The Department sends an electronic Determination letter to the local authority confirming the provision of the new powers and the Minister writes to the local MPs and the Leader of the Council informing them of the date when the powers will come into effect.	
12) The CPE powers come into effect.	

Application for Civil Parking Enforcement and Bus Lane Enforcement

> **** Council
>
> **** on behalf of **** Council
>
> **** month/year ****

Introduction

State here whether the Council intends to use these powers from the outset of civil enforcement coming into effect.

> This document represents the formal application from **** Council **** on behalf of **** Council **** for civil parking enforcement (CPE) powers under the provisions of Part Six of the Traffic Management Act 2004.
>
> The Council wishes to apply for a Civil Enforcement Area (CEA) and a Special Enforcement Area (SEA).
>
> This document also represents the Council's application for bus lane enforcement powers under the provisions of the Transport Act 2000.

Proposed commencement date

State proposed commencement date. Council should first seek agreement from an official at the Department for Transport of the proposed CPE date.

Definition of CEA/SEA and excluded roads

Provide in plain English a clear and accurate description of the area excluded from the CEA /SEA and also explain the area that is included within the CEA.

Confirmation required that all off-street car parks owned by the district(s)/ borough(s) council(s) are included within the proposed CEA/SEA.

If military roads are not defined within the excluded routes the Department requires confirmation that this is the case.

Map

Include a detailed map of the proposed CEA/SEA and all of the excluded roads at Appendix A.

TRO confirmation

Formal confirmation of the state of the TROs, signs, lines and road markings MUST be confirmed by a senior Council official six weeks prior to the CPE commencement date. A formal letter to the Department should be drafted along the following lines:

1) A complete review of the Traffic Regulation Orders (TROs), traffic signs and road markings within the council's entire proposed Civil Enforcement Area/Special Enforcement Area has taken place in order to highlight any deficiencies.

2) Any deficiencies highlighted as part of this review have been rectified.

3) As a result of this work, all TROs, traffic signs and road markings within the entire proposed CEA/SEA conform to the legislation and are consistent with one another.

4) This requirement extends to all TROs, traffic signs and road markings with no exceptions and therefore includes existing, new and replacement TROs, traffic signs and road markings.

Signed: _____

Printed: _____

Position: _____

Dated: _____

Alteration of equipment

The Council should ensure that all pay-and-display equipment, including all parking meters, are altered to use the term 'penalty' instead of 'initial' or 'excess' no later than six months after the introduction of CPE.

Parking management strategies and policies

Provide a summary of the Council's parking management strategy as set out in the Council's LTP.

Application for a CEA designation order – March 2008

Parking management review

Outline the scope of the parking management review that has taken place as a result of current enforcement problems and the impending introduction of CPE.

Civil Parking Enforcement

Explain the current level of parking provision in place for both on and off-street.

The enforcement picture after the introduction of CPE

Explain why the introduction of CPE will help to improve parking management within the Council's administrative area.

Include a paragraph here outlining the projected levels of parking provision both on and off-street in the five year period that will follow the introduction of CPE.

Financial assessment

Provide confirmation here that the Council has considered the financial implication of CPE.

A full financial assessment should be included at Appendix B and this should incorporate an assessment of income and expenditure during the first five years of CPE. Any significant changes in financial performance expected in the following years should also be noted.

Documentation

Explain here who will be responsible for providing and designing the necessary documentation (i.e. forms, notices, letters, PCNs, NtOs and Charge Certificates).

Notice processing

Who will be responsible for processing the notices?

Contravention codes

Which version will be implemented?

PCN numbering system

Confirm the PCN numbering system

Civil Enforcement Officers

Explain how many CEOs will be required and how they will be deployed on and off-street.

Training

Include a section here detailing the extent of the training that will be provided for existing and newly recruited Civil Enforcement Officers.

Uniforms

Describe what type of uniform will be worn by CEOs, how will CEOs be identified from other CEOs and confirm whether they will be carrying or wearing an ID.

Equipment

Describe the equipment that CEOs will be provided with for the purposes of communication.

PCNs

Penalty Charge levels

Include a description of the Penalty Charge levels that will be used from the outset of the Council's CPE scheme. This should include the penalty charge level that is applicable at all of the stages after the PCN is first issued, and whether any variable charge levels will apply.

Payment methods

Include a bullet point section here detailing the range of payment facilities that will be available to customers.

Exemptions and dispensation notices

What type of vehicles or group of individuals will be eligible for exemptions?

Include descriptions here of how the system of exemptions/dispensation notices will work in practice for each vehicle type/group of individuals.

Pavement parking

What plans, if any, does the Council have to enforce pavement parking contravention.

Dropped-kerb parking

Explain the Council's plans to enforce parking contraventions at dropped kerbs (if any).

Double parking

Explain the Council's plans to enforce parking contraventions more than 50 cm from the kerb (if any).

Vehicle immobilisation and removals

Explain the Council's policy on the practice of vehicle immobilisation as a measure for enforcing parking contraventions and at what stage is the Council intending to implement immobilisation. State whether the Council will comply with TMA regulations and guidelines.

Explain whether the Council intends to use vehicle removal as an enforcement measure from the outset of the introduction of CPE. Also state whether the Council will comply with current TMA regulations and guidance accordingly.

Representations and appeals

Informal representations

Council are now obliged to consider informal representations and should set out how they propose to deal with them, including the processes associated with this form of appeal.

Formal representations

Detail the format in which formal representations will be accepted and handled (i.e. whether representations will be dealt with by post/and or electronically).

Adjudications

Confirm whether the Council has joined the Traffic Penalty Tribunal (TPT) and applied for the necessary powers to undertake adjudications.

Confirm the venue/venues that will be used for carrying out adjudication services and provide evidence that TPT have approved the venue.

PCN recovery

Provide evidence that the Council has liaised with both the Driver Vehicle and Licensing Agency (DVLA) and the Traffic Enforcement Centre (TEC), and append consultation responses confirming that both agencies are content with the Council's arrangements for the requesting of information on registered vehicle keepers and for requesting the registration of charge certificates and the granting of authority to prepare warrants of execution.

Publicity

Describe in bullet form the different elements that will be included within the publicity programme for the implementation of CPE. When will the publicity be conducted and for what length of period.

Consultation

List all the consultees with regard to the introduction of CPE Powers.

The following MUST be consulted:

Neighbouring local authorities
Police
Highways Agency
DVLA and TEC
Government Office
Traffic Penalty Tribunal (TPT)

Statistics collection

The Council must confirm that it will report annually to the Secretary of State on the financial results of civil parking enforcement, and any action the Council takes in respect of any deficit or surplus on the on-street parking account.

Legal documentation

The Council must supply evidence of its current legal name(s) along with the legal names of the borough(s)/district(s) where CPE will be introduced.

Appendix A – Map

Attach a detailed map of the entire area covered by the CEA/SEA here, including a list of all the excluded roads.

Appendix B – Financial assessment

Attach a copy of the Council's full financial assessment here.

Appendix C – Consultation

Attach copies of consultation documents here. All consultation responses should indicate that the party consulted is content with the Council's application and that any contentious issues have been fully resolved.

Consultation responses from the DVLA, TPT and the TEC should all include details of the arrangements that have been made/need to be made between the Council and the relevant body prior to the introduction of CPE.

Appendix D – Legal name(s)

Confirm the Council's legal name here and include a copy extract from the appropriate legal instrument or resolution that grants the Council its name in law. Where a county council is applying on behalf of one or more borough or district councils, confirm the legal names and include copy extracts from the appropriate legal instruments or resolutions for all of these councils.

Attach a copy of the Council's resolution to take up CPE powers here. Where a county council is applying on behalf of one or more borough or district councils, include copies of the appropriate resolutions for all of the councils.

Appendix E – Contact details

Insert the contact details (i.e. telephone numbers and email addresses) for the officials who have commented on this application form:

Police
The Highways Agency
Government Office

Insert the postal address details for the Leader of the Council and all of the local MPs here (these officials will be sent confirmation letters once the proposed commencement date has been fixed).

ANNEX A
What the civil enforcement of parking under the Traffic Management Act 2004 involves and how it differs from decriminalised parking enforcement under the Road Traffic Act 1991

What CPE involves

A1 The regulations made under Part 6 of the Traffic Management Act 2004 enable an authority in England, once they have been given the relevant power by the Secretary of State, to enforce parking contraventions within a particular geographical area.

- Enforcement primarily becomes the responsibility of the authority but the police remain responsible for endorseable offences such as dangerous parking, obstruction, failure to comply with police 'no parking' signs placed in emergencies, and any vehicle where security or other traffic policing issues are involved, including the need to close roads or set up diversions. Stopping offences at pedestrian crossings or zigzag lines may be enforced by the police or the authority, but police action takes precedence.

- Civil Enforcement Officers (CEOs) employed directly or indirectly by the local authority place Penalty Charge Notices (PCNs) on vehicles contravening parking restrictions and, when appropriately trained and entitled, can authorise the immobilisation or removal of vehicles.

- If the penalty charge remains unpaid after the relevant time and processes, it becomes a civil debt due to the authority and enforceable through a streamlined version of the normal civil debt recovery process in the county court.

- A motorist wishing to contest liability for a penalty charge may make representations to the authority and, if these are rejected, may have grounds to appeal to an independent adjudicator. The adjudicator's decision may be reconsidered by another adjudicator but there is no right of further appeal through the courts except to the High Court on an application for judicial review of the adjudicator's decision.

- The enforcement authority keeps any proceeds from penalty charges, which finance the enforcement and adjudication systems. Authorities must only use any financial surpluses from on-street parking charges and on- and off-street penalty charges for the purposes set out in section 55 (as amended)[182] of the RTRA and authorities need to keep separate accounts of PCN income from on-street enforcement and from off-street enforcement.

---

[182] S.I. 2007/3482, regulations 25 and 26

- The system of 'initial' and 'excess' charges for paid parking that are used by local authorities when on-street parking is enforced by the police service do not apply.

- Outside the areas where authorities are responsible for civil parking enforcement all parking offences will remain subject to the criminal law.

A2 The main advantages of civil parking enforcement are:

- authorities can ensure that their parking policies are implemented effectively, with improved traffic flow, better management of overall traffic levels, fewer accidents, a fairer distribution of available parking places and a more pleasant environment;

- integration of enforcement and parking policy responsibilities should provide better monitoring of the effectiveness and value of parking controls, so that parking provision becomes more responsive to the public's needs; and

- authorities may use any revenue from parking charges and penalty charges to fund enforcement activities. They can use any surpluses to improve off-street parking, or, where this is unnecessary or undesirable, for certain other transport-related purposes and environmental schemes.

Civil Enforcement Areas

A3 Schedule 8 of the Traffic Management Act 2004 enables an eligible local authority to apply to the Secretary of State for an order creating a 'Civil Enforcement Area' (CEA). CEAs replace the 'Permitted Parking Areas' (PPAs) and 'Special Parking Areas' (SPAs) created under the Road Traffic Act 1991. All existing PPAs/SPAs automatically become CEAs under the TMA.

A4 Within a CEA, contraventions of Orders designating permitted on-street parking places, such as meter bays, residents' and disabled persons' bays and free parking bays, are subject to civil enforcement by the local authority.

A5 There is a civilly enforceable parking contravention in relation to a vehicle if the vehicle is stationary in a parking place anywhere in Greater London and:

(a) the vehicle has been left;

(i) otherwise than as authorised by or under any order relating to the parking place; or

(ii) beyond the period of parking that has been paid for;

(b) no parking charge payable with respect to the vehicle has been paid; or

(c) there has been, with respect to the vehicle, a contravention of any provision made by or under any order relating to the parking place.

For this purpose 'parking place' means:

(a) a parking place designated by an order made under section 6, 9 or 45 of the Road Traffic Regulation Act 1984 (c. 27); or

(b) an off-street parking place provided under section 32(1)(a) of that Act.

A6 The following contraventions are also civilly enforceable if committed in a civil enforcement area in Greater London in relation to a stationary vehicle:

(a) an offence under section 15 of the Greater London Council (General Powers) Act 1974 (parking on footways, verges, etc.);

(b) an offence under section 8, 11, 16(1) or 16C of the Road Traffic Regulation Act 1984 (contravention of certain traffic orders) of contravening:

(i) a prohibition or restriction on waiting of vehicles; or

(ii) provision relating to any of the matters mentioned in paragraph 7 or 8 of Schedule 1 to that Act (conditions for loading or unloading, or delivering or collecting);

(c) an offence under section 25(5) of the Road Traffic Regulation Act 1984 of contravening regulation 18 or 20 of the Zebra, Pelican and Puffin Pedestrian Crossings Regulations and General Directions 1997 (S.I. 1997/2400) (prohibition on stopping vehicles on or near pedestrian crossings);

(d) an offence under section 35A(1) of the Road Traffic Regulation Act 1984 (contravention of orders relating to parking places provided under section 32 or 33 of that Act);

(e) an offence under section 61(5) of the Road Traffic Regulation Act 1984 (parking in loading areas);

(f) an offence under section 19 of the Road Traffic Act 1988 (parking of HGVs on verges, central reservations or footways);

(g) an offence under section 21 of the Road Traffic Act 1988 (offences relating to cycle tracks) of parking a vehicle wholly or partly on a cycle track;

(h) an offence under section 36(1) of the Road Traffic Act 1988 (failure to comply with traffic sign) of failing to comply with a sign of a type referred to in:

(i) regulation 10(1)(b) of the Traffic Signs Regulations and General Directions 2002 (S.I. 2002/3113) (zig-zag lines relating to certain crossings); or

(ii) regulation 29(1) of those regulations (bus stop or bus stand markings).

A7 Outside Greater London the following contraventions are civilly enforceable if committed in relation to a stationary vehicle:

(a) an offence under section 64(3) of the Local Government (Miscellaneous Provisions) Act 1976 (c. 57) of causing a vehicle to stop on part of a road appointed, or deemed to have been appointed, as a hackney carriage stand;

(b) an offence under section 5, 11, 16(1) or 16C of the Road Traffic Regulation Act 1984 (c. 27) (contravention of certain traffic orders) of contravening a prohibition or restriction on waiting, or loading or unloading, of vehicles;

(c) an offence under section 25(5) of the Road Traffic Regulation Act 1984 of contravening regulation 18 or 20 of the Zebra, Pelican and Puffin Pedestrian Crossings Regulations and General Directions 1997 (S.I. 1997/2400) (prohibition on stopping vehicles on or near pedestrian crossings);

(d) an offence under section 35A(1), 47(1) or 53(5) or (6) of the Road Traffic Regulation Act 1984 (offences in connection with parking places);

(e) an offence under section 61(5) of the Road Traffic Regulation Act 1984 (parking in loading areas);

(f) an offence under section 6(6) of the Essex Act 1987 (c. xx) of leaving a vehicle on any land in contravention of a prohibition under that section (prohibitions relating to verges and certain other land adjoining or accessible from highway);

(g) an offence under section 19 of the Road Traffic Act 1988 (parking of HGVs on verges, central reservations or footways);

(h) an offence under section 21 of the Road Traffic Act 1988 (offences relating to cycle tracks) of parking a vehicle wholly or partly on a cycle track;

(i) an offence under section 36(1) of the Road Traffic Act 1988 (failure to comply with traffic sign) of failing to comply with a sign of a type referred to in:

  (i) regulation 10(1)(b) of the Traffic Signs Regulations and General Directions 2002 (S.I. 2002/3113) (zig-zag lines relating to certain crossings), or

  (ii) regulation 29(1) of those regulations (bus stop or bus stand markings).

A8 In accordance with regulation 7 of the Civil Enforcement of Parking Contraventions (England) General Regulations 2007 (S.I. 2007/3483), with one exception, no criminal proceedings may be brought and no fixed penalty notice may be given in respect of any of these contraventions. The exception is a 'pedestrian crossing contravention', that is one of the offences referred to in subparagraph (c) or (h)(i) of paragraph A6 or subparagraph (c) or (i)(i) of paragraph A7. If criminal proceedings are started or a fixed penalty notice is given for one of those offences then no penalty charge is payable under the Traffic Management Act 2004 or regulations made under it and, if a penalty charge is paid, it must be refunded as soon as reasonably practicable after the circumstances come to light.

Special Enforcement Areas

A9 The TMA enables authorities with CPE power to enforce in a Special Enforcement Area (SEA)[183] prohibitions of double parking[184] and parking at dropped footways[185] as if they had been introduced using a Traffic Regulation Order (Traffic Management Order in London). Any Special Parking Area that existed before commencement of the TMA 2004 automatically becomes an SEA[186] and outside London the restrictions need to be indicated with traffic signs or road markings. In London the provisions remain in force in local Acts of Parliament that mean traffic signs and road markings are not required. Authorities should make sure that the public are aware of the new restrictions before starting enforcement.

How CPE differs from DPE

A10 The arrangements under Part 6 of the Traffic Management Act 2004 largely replicate and update those under Part II of the Road Traffic Act 1991.

Presentational

- Decriminalised Parking Enforcement to be called Civil Parking Enforcement.
- Parking Attendants to be called Civil Enforcement Officers.
- Special Parking Areas and Permitted Parking Areas to be called Civil Enforcement Areas.

Changes to regulations (and, therefore, to Guidance)

All English authorities:

- Different parking penalties depending on the seriousness of the contravention.
- Details of procedures for representations and appeals on PCN.
- Power to serve PCNs by post if CEO has started to issue it but motorist leaves with the vehicle before it can be served.
- Enforcement cameras ('approved devices') to be certified by the Secretary of State.
- 21 day discount for PCNs sent by post with evidence from an approved device.
- Authorities must not immobilise within 30 minutes of the issue of a PCN in a parking place, with the exception of persistent evaders who may be clamped after 15 minutes of the issue of the PCN.
- Authorities must consider informal representations.
- Procedures to reissue Notices if payments cancelled after payment.
- Authorities must decide representations within 56 days.

---

[183] Traffic Management Act 2004, Schedule 10

[184] *Ibid*, section 85

[185] *Ibid*, section 86

[186] *Ibid*, schedule 10, Paragraphs 2(5) and 3(5)

- Adjudicators have the power to decide cases where procedural irregularity has taken place (for example, where a Charge Certificate has been issued before an appeal has been decided).
- Adjudicators have the power to refer back to the authority for reconsideration cases where a contravention took place but in mitigating circumstances.

New powers and duties for authorities outside London currently only held by those in London enable them to:

- send PCNs by post with camera evidence;
- send PCNs by post when prevented from serving by violence;
- enforce dropped footways in an SEA;
- enforce double parking in an SEA; and
- place a six month time limit on authorities serving a Notice to Owner.

Changes to Guidance

- Authorities no longer need to demonstrate to the Secretary of State that parking enforcement would be self-funding.
- Authorities should publish parking policies.
- In situations where a contravention has occurred but in mitigating circumstances authorities should make and publish guidelines on their use of discretion which should be applied flexibly.
- Stronger emphasis on staff training.
- Authorities are encouraged to use photographic evidence obtained by CEOs as additional evidence that the contravention has occurred.
- Discouragement to immobilise vehicles except those of persistent evaders.
- Where a vehicle is parked in contravention and in an obstructive manner the vehicle should be removed rather than immobilised.
- Where an informal challenge made against a PCN within the 14 day 50 per cent discount period is rejected, authorities encouraged to re-offer discount.
- Authorities should review their parking policies on a regular basis in consultation with local stakeholders and, once finalised, these should be made publicly available in an annual report.
- Authorities should publish certain items of financial and statistical information.
- More emphasis on monitoring.

ANNEX B
Enforcement action started under the Road Traffic Act 1991

B1 Until 2400 hours on Sunday 30 March 2008, enforcement action should be taken using the powers in the Road Traffic Act 1991 or other relevant legislation. From 00.00.01 hours on Monday 31 March 2008 enforcement action should be taken under the Traffic Management Act 2004 and the associated regulations.

B2 Any enforcement action in respect of a parking contravention observed or detected before 2400 hours on Sunday 30 March 2008 must be taken using the powers in RTA 1991 and other legislation. For instance, the PCN for a contravention in London at 2200 hours detected with cameras and served on 31 March must be served under the legislation that was in force when the contravention took place. Further action (NtO, NoR, Charge Certificate, appeals, etc.) in respect of a PCN issued under the RTA 1991 or other legislation must be taken using the RTA 1991 or the legislation under which the PCN was served.

B3 This means that enforcement authorities, the TEC, bailiffs and the adjudicators must run two systems until there is no possibility of subsequent action being taken in respect of a PCN served under the RTA 1991 or the other legislation that is repealed.

ANNEX C
Contraventions for which the higher and the lower level penalty charges should be made

* = or other specified time   **** = or other number   † = or other specified distance

Higher level contraventions

On-street

Code	Description
01	Parked in a restricted street during prescribed hours
02	Parked or loading/unloading in a restricted street where waiting and loading/unloading restrictions are in force
12	Parked in a residents' or shared use parking place without clearly displaying either a permit or voucher or pay and display ticket issued for that place
14	Parked in an electric vehicles' charging place during restricted hours without charging
16	Parked in a permit space without displaying a valid permit
18	Using a vehicle in a parking place in connection with the sale or offering or exposing for sale of goods when prohibited
20	Parked in a loading gap marked by a yellow line
21	Parked in a suspended bay/space or part of bay/space
23	Parked in a parking place or area not designated for that class of vehicle
25	Parked in a loading place during restricted hours without loading
26	Vehicle parked more than 50 centimetres from the edge of the carriageway and not within a designated parking place
27	Parked adjacent to a dropped footway
40	Parked in a designated disabled person's parking place without clearly displaying a valid disabled person's badge
41	Parked in a parking place designated for diplomatic vehicles
42	Parked in a parking place designated for police vehicles
45	Parked on a taxi rank
46	Stopped where prohibited (on a red route or clearway)
47	Stopped on a restricted bus stop or stand
48	Stopped in a restricted area outside a school
49	Parked wholly or partly on a cycle track

Code	Description
55	A commercial vehicle parked in a restricted street in contravention of the overnight waiting ban
56	Parked in contravention of a commercial vehicle waiting restriction
57	Parked in contravention of a coach ban
61	A heavy commercial vehicle wholly or partly parked on a footway, verge or land between two carriageways
62	Parked with one or more wheels on any part of an urban road other than a carriageway (footway parking)
99	Stopped on a pedestrian crossing and/or crossing area marked by zig-zags

Off-street

Code	Description
70	Parked in a loading area during restricted hours without reasonable excuse
74	Using a vehicle in a parking place in connection with the sale or offering or exposing for sale of goods when prohibited
81	Parked in a restricted area in a car park
85	Parked in a permit bay without clearly displaying a valid permit
87	Parked in a disabled person's parking space without clearly displaying a valid disabled person's badge
89	Vehicle parked exceeds maximum weight and/or height and/or length permitted in the area
91	Parked in a car park or area not designated for that class of vehicle
92	Parked causing an obstruction

Lower level contraventions

On-street

Code	Description
04	Parked in a meter bay when penalty time is indicated
05	Parked after the expiry of paid for time
06	Parked without clearly displaying a valid pay-and-display ticket or voucher
07	Parked with payment made to extend the stay beyond initial time
08	Parked at an out-of-order meter during controlled hours
09	Parked displaying multiple pay-and-display tickets where prohibited
10	Parked without clearly displaying two**** valid pay-and-display tickets when required
11	Parked without payment of the parking charge
19	Parked in a residents' or shared use parking place or zone displaying an invalid permit, an invalid voucher or an invalid pay-and-display ticket
22	Re-parked in the same parking place within one hour* of leaving

Code	Description
24	Not parked correctly within the markings of the bay or space
30	Parked for longer than permitted
35	Parked in a disc parking place without clearly displaying a valid disc
36	Parked in a disc parking place for longer than permitted
63	Parked with engine running where prohibited

Off-street

Code	Description
73	Parked without payment of the parking charge
80	Parked for longer than the maximum period permitted
82	Parked after the expiry of paid for time
83	Parked in a car park without clearly displaying a valid pay-and-display ticket or voucher or parking clock
84	Parked with additional payment made to extend the stay beyond time first purchased
86	Parked beyond the bay markings
90	Re-parked within one hour* of leaving a bay or space in a car park
93	Parked in car park when closed
94	Parked in a pay-and-display car park without clearly displaying two**** valid pay-and-display tickets when required
95	Parked in a parking place for a purpose other than the designated purpose for the parking place
96	Parked with engine running where prohibited

Annex C – March 2008

ANNEX D
Examples of information that it may be prudent for a CEO to note

- Postcode of street (particularly if more than one street with the same name in an area or if a common street name).

- Confirmation that PCN affixed to vehicle, handed to motorist or to be posted (this information may be useful in case a motorist subsequently denies knowledge of the PCN). If CEOs have a digital camera, a picture of the vehicle with the PCN attached will be useful evidence if the motorist claims that it was not served. Such a claim is not likely to be made in many cases but it may be prudent to take such photographs in areas or on occasions when the removal of PCNs by strangers from vehicles is prevalent.

- Numbers of any other PCNs – to prevent more than one PCN being issued on the same day when the vehicle has not been moved.

- Any permit, badge, voucher or pay-and-display ticket displayed.

- Pocket book reference number and page number (if applicable).

- Tyre valve positions and whether off side or near side.

- Whether clamping or removal has been requested by the CEO.

- Class of VED licence (for example, PLG, HGV).

- Expiry date of excise licence (for reporting to DVLA and/or possibly abandoned vehicles team when out of date).

- Whether PCN spoilt and whether it was re-issued.

- Taking photos before and after serving the PCN if CEO likely to serve ticket

Loading or unloading

- Loading or unloading seen (for example, if loading seen earlier in day, but not taking place when PCN issued, or if loading taking place when prohibited).

- Length of observation period and whether continuous or casual.

Foreign or diplomatic plates

- Foreign or diplomatic plates (to highlight use of special procedures for processing diplomats' PCNs).

Conversation with motorist, breakdowns, drive aways etc

- Driver seen (time and other details) or vehicle otherwise occupied.

- Description of person who appeared to be in charge of the vehicle if seen.

- Conversation with driver or other person with/in the vehicle (time and other details).
- Details of any note displayed on windscreen.
- Evidence of any breakdown.

Prohibited parking

- Details of yellow/red lines/kerb stripes (for example single, double line/ one, two kerb stripes).
- Details of kerbside plates (for example position relative to the vehicle, times of loading and waiting restrictions).
- Detailed location of vehicle (for example by/on N/S/E/W kerb; outside/ opposite No.; X yards N/S/E/W of junction with Y Road).
- In yellow/redline cases, CEOs should record as much information as possible to establish the precise location of the vehicle, especially in streets where there may be a range of different regulations in different parts.

Permitted parking

- Expiry time of pay-and-display ticket or voucher (if appropriate).
- Parking zone/parking place identifier.
- Details of signs and their position relative to the vehicle.
- Details of vehicle location (for example, outside or opposite an address).
- If prohibited, whether meter feeding detected and details.
- If meter or machine out of order.
- Display on meter/machine if not just penalty time (for example Out Of Order/ No parking until…).
- On pay-and-display machines, time shown on machine compared to time on PA's watch or HHC.
- Details of any suspension.

Inadequate markings or signs etc.

- Details of any inadequacies in road markings.
- Details of any damage to kerbside plates or missing plates.
- Damaged street furniture or any other heath and safety issues.

ANNEX E
Appraising the adequacy of traffic signs, plating and road markings

E1 All local authorities are responsible for the accuracy and condition of the traffic signs and road markings that identify parking restrictions in their area. The traffic signs and road markings must conform strictly to the relevant regulations (currently the Traffic Signs Regulations and General Directions 2002 – TSRGD – and subsequent amendments) or have special authorisation from DfT. They should also conform to the guidance set out in Chapters 3 and 5 of the Traffic Signs Manual.

E2 PCNs may not be valid if they are issued where traffic signs and road markings are incorrect or in poor condition. Representations demonstrating this should be accepted. If such representations are not accepted, any subsequent appeal may be successful. Authorities should, therefore, have the services of an employee or contractor who is capable of reading and applying TSRGD 2002 and the Traffic Signs Manual. When the Institute of Highway Engineers (IHIE) qualification in traffic sign design is in place, the employee or contractor should have achieved at least 'practitioner' level.

E3 Before applying for the new powers, as part of their review of existing TROs (see Chapter 13), authorities should ensure that the relevant traffic signs and road markings are present and:

- consistent with TSRGD;
- in a good state of repair; and
- that their meaning will be clear to visitors as well as local people.

E4 Authorities will have to confirm in writing that this has been done before the Secretary of State will ask Parliament to give them enforcement powers.

E5 The Secretary of State's view is that motorists cannot reasonably be expected to read, understand and remember the parking restrictions at the entrance to a Controlled Parking Zone that covers an area of more than a dozen streets. CPZs rely solely on zone entry signs to give times of operation and to remove the need for time plates within the zone, except on lengths of road where the restrictions apply at different times to the rest of the zone. The area of a CPZ should, therefore, be restricted to, for example, a town centre shopping area. A single zone covering a whole town, or suburb of a conurbation, would be much too large. Conventional time plate signing, without zone entry signs, should accompany the yellow sign markings where large areas have waiting restrictions. Time plates are not necessary where there are double yellow lines.

E6 Where CPZ (or Restricted Parking Zone – RPZ – where authorised) signing is to be used, care should be taken when siting the zone entry signs to ensure that they are clearly and safely visible to motorists. Unless unavoidable, they should not be close to junctions on busy roads, where motorists are likely to be concentrating on direction signs, traffic lights and other directional manoeuvring. Locations where the zone entry signs are likely to be obscured by large vehicles (for example, delivery vans, or buses at bus stops) should also be avoided. Local authorities will also need to ensure that they do not become obscured by vegetation or street furniture, including other traffic signs.

E7 In areas of the greatest sensitivity there may be ways of balancing the need for clear signs against visual intrusion.

Maintenance of signs, meters, and the like

E8 Chapter 6 says that CEOs may be given the task of checking and reporting on the state of signs, plating, markings, parking meters, pay-and-display machines, and the like as one of their patrol duties. It might also be appropriate for officers to carry out certain minor repairs to meters and pay-and-display machines. However, it will be for the authority concerned to arrange for any major defects to be rectified, either by its own staff or a contractor.

ANNEX F
Appraising Traffic Regulation Orders (TROs) and Traffic Management Orders (TMOs)

F1 The foundation of an effective parking enforcement regime is lawful and up-to-date Traffic Regulation Orders (TROs). In London, these are called Traffic Management Orders (TMOs) and can be made for a slightly wider range of purposes. The Road Traffic Regulation Act 1984 gives local traffic authorities wide powers to make TROs or TMOs on the roads for which they are responsible. The Secretary of State has similar powers for trunk roads.

F2 This annex summarises the generally applicable requirements and procedures for making orders and the specific arrangements for review when adopting civil enforcement powers. This guidance is based on the current legislation as described in the footnotes.

Permanent TROs

F3 A TRO may only be made for the following purposes:[187]

- avoiding danger to persons or traffic (including for anti-terrorist purposes);
- preventing damage to the road or to buildings nearby (including for anti-terrorist purposes);
- facilitating the passage of traffic;
- preventing use by unsuitable traffic;
- preserving the character of a road especially suitable for walking or horse riding;
- preserving or improving amenities of the area through which the road runs; and
- for any of the purposes specified in paragraphs (a) to (c) of the Environment Act 1995 (air quality).

F4 To meet one or more of the above, a TRO may prohibit, restrict or regulate the use of a road or any part of the width of a road by vehicular traffic of any class. It may have effect at all times or at specified periods or times. Specific classes of traffic may be excepted. A TRO can:[188]

- require all or specified classes of vehicular traffic to proceed in a specified direction or prohibit it from so proceeding;
- specify the part of the carriageway to be used by such traffic proceeding in a specified direction;

---

187 Road Traffic Regulation Act 1984, section 1(1)
188 *Ibid*, section 2

- prohibit or restrict the waiting of vehicles or the loading and unloading of vehicles;
- prohibit the use of roads by through traffic;
- prohibit or restrict overtaking.

F5 A TRO can specify through routes for heavy vehicles, or prohibit or restrict their use in specified roads or zones in order to preserve or improve amenities in the area.

F6 A TRO can regulate the use of a road by pedestrians[189] but must not have the effect of preventing pedestrian access at any time, or preventing vehicular access for more than 8 hours in 24, to premises on or adjacent to the road. However, the restriction on vehicular access does not apply if the local authority states in the order that they are satisfied that it should not so as to:

- avoid danger to persons or other traffic using the road to which the order relates or any other road;
- prevent the likelihood of any such danger arising;
- prevent damage to the road or buildings on or near it;
- facilitate the passage of vehicular traffic on the road; and
- preserve or improve the amenities of an area by prohibiting or restricting the use on a road or roads in that area of heavy commercial vehicles.

Permanent TMOs

F7 In London, an authority can also make a TMO in the following circumstances:[190]

- For prescribing the routes to be followed by all classes of traffic, or by any class or classes of traffic, from one specified point to another, either generally or between any specified times.
- For prescribing streets which are not to be used for traffic by vehicles, or by vehicles of any specified class or classes, either generally or at specified times.
- For regulating the relative position in the roadway of traffic of differing speeds or types.
- For prescribing the places where vehicles, or vehicles of any class, may not turn so as to face in the opposite direction to that in which they were proceeding, or where they may only so turn under conditions prescribed by the order.
- For prescribing the conditions subject to which, and the times at which, articles of exceptionally heavy weight or exceptionally large dimensions may be carried by road.

---

189 *Ibid*, section 3

190 *Ibid*, section 6 and Schedule 1

- For prescribing the number and maximum size and weight of trailers which may be drawn on streets by vehicles, or by vehicles of any class, either generally or on streets of any class or description, and for prescribing that a man should be carried on the trailer or, where more than one trailer is drawn, on the rear trailer for signalling to the driver.

- For prescribing the conditions subject to which, and the times at which, articles may be loaded on to or unloaded from vehicles, or vehicles of any class, on streets.

- For prescribing the conditions subject to which, and the times at which, vehicles, or vehicles of any class, delivering or collecting goods or merchandise, or delivering goods or merchandise of any particular class, may stand in streets, or in streets of any class or description, or in specified streets.

- For prescribing the conditions subject to which, and the times at which, vehicles, or vehicles of any class, may be used on streets for collecting refuse.

- For prescribing rules as to precedence to be observed as between vehicles proceeding in the same direction, in opposite directions, or when crossing.

- For prescribing the conditions subject to which, and the times at which, horses, cattle, sheep and other animals may be led or driven on streets within Greater London.

- For requiring the erection, exhibition or removal of traffic notices, and as to the form, plan and character of such notices.

- Broken down vehicles.

- Vehicles, or vehicles of any class, when unattended.

- Places in streets where vehicles, or vehicles of any class, may, or may not, wait, either generally or at particular times.

- Cabs and hackney carriages not hired and being in a street elsewhere than on a cab rank.

- For restricting the use of vehicles and animals, and sandwich-board men and other persons, in streets for the purposes of advertisement of such a nature or in such a manner as is to be likely to be a source of danger or to cause obstruction to traffic.

- The lighting and guarding of street works.

- The erection or placing or the removal of any works or objects likely to hinder the free circulation of traffic in any street or likely to cause danger to passengers or vehicles.

- Queues of persons waiting in streets.

- Priority of entry to public vehicles.

- For enabling any police, local or other public authority to do anything which under the order a person ought to have done and has failed to do, and to recover from the person so in default, summarily as a civil debt, the expenses of doing it.

Experimental orders

F8 A traffic authority may test a scheme of traffic control, normally for up to 18 months, using an 'experimental traffic order' before deciding whether to make it permanent.[191]

F9 An authority should put robust arrangements in place to measure the traffic situation before and after introduction of the experimental measure and monitor its effect. This should help avoid accusations that the authority has used an experimental order to avoid the procedure requirements of a permanent one. Substantial capital investment in the measures introduced by an experimental TRO is likely to undermine public confidence in its investigative nature.

Parking designation orders

F10 Local authorities may, for the purpose of relieving or preventing congestion of traffic, provide suitable parking places on a highway for vehicles or vehicles of any class.[192] Similarly, they can designate highway parking places for vehicles of any class (and subject to conditions of use) for which a charge may be made when used.[193]

Traffic signs and devices used to control waiting restrictions

F11 TROs and TMOs may specify authorised traffic signs to identify the traffic regulation involved.[194]

F12 A TRO or TMO that imposes any restriction on the use by vehicles of a road, or the waiting of vehicles in a road, may include provision with respect to the issue and display of certificates or other means of identification of vehicles which are exempted from the restriction.[195]

F13 A TRO or TMO may include provisions on the issue, display and operation of devices for indicating the time at which a vehicle arrived at, and the time at which it ought to leave, any place in a road in which waiting is restricted.[196]

---

191 *Ibid*, section 9
192 *Ibid*, section 32
193 *Ibid*, section 45
194 *Ibid*, sections 4(1) and 7(1)
195 *Ibid*, sections 4(2) and 7(2)
196 *Ibid*, sections 4(3) and 7(3)

TROs for special areas in the countryside

F14 TROs can be made for roads in special areas of the countryside (such as National Parks) for the purposes of conserving or enhancing the natural beauty of the area or of affording better opportunities for the public to enjoy its amenities, including for recreation or the study of nature.[197]

Temporary prohibitions and restrictions

F15 Where a traffic authority is satisfied that traffic on a road should be restricted or prohibited:

- because works are being or are proposed to be executed on or near the road; or
- because of the likelihood of danger to the public, or of serious damage to the road, which is not attributable to such works; or
- for the purpose of litter clearance and cleaning in accordance with section 89(1)(a) or (2) of the Environmental Protection Act 1990

it may, by temporary order, restrict or prohibit the use of the road, or of any part of it, by vehicles of any class, or by pedestrians, as they consider necessary.[198]

F16 A temporary restriction cannot normally remain in force for more than six months if it is in respect of a footpath, bridleway, cycle track or byway open to all traffic, and for more than 18 months in any other case. (The 18-month limit does not apply where an authority is satisfied, and it is stated in the order that it is satisfied, that works in question will take longer, provided that the authority then revokes the order as soon as the works have been completed).

F17 The authority must consult the National Park authority for any National Park which would be affected by the order.

F18 Where the traffic authority is satisfied that the works, danger, or litter clearance should come into force without delay, the temporary restriction or prohibition may be imposed by notice.

Special events

F19 If the traffic authority is satisfied that traffic should be restricted or prohibited in connection with a sporting event, social event or entertainment which is held on a road, it may by order restrict or prohibit temporarily the use of that road to such extent and subject to such conditions or exceptions as they consider necessary or expedient.[199] (Such regulation is permitted to: facilitate the holding of the event; or enable members of the public to watch

---

[197] *Ibid*, section 22

[198] *Ibid*, section 14

[199] *Ibid*, section 16A

the event; or to reduce the disruption to traffic likely to be caused by the event). Before making such an order, the authority must be satisfied that it is not reasonably practicable for the event to be held otherwise than on a road; and the authority must have regard to the safety and convenience of alternative routes suitable for the traffic which will be affected by the order.

F20 This sort of order cannot be made in relation to any race or trial falling within subsection (1) of section 12 of the Road Traffic Act 1988 (motor racing on public ways); nor in relation to any competition or trial falling within subsection (1) of section 13 of that Act (regulation of motoring events on public ways) unless the competition or trial is authorised by or under regulations under that section; nor in relation to any race or trial falling within subsection (1) of section 31 of that Act (regulation of cycle racing on public ways) unless the race or trial is authorised by or under regulations made under that section.

F21 In London there are specific provisions and procedures for imposing temporary waiting prohibitions in connection with such an event and the holding of funerals.[200]

F22 Unlike for permanent orders and certain other types of temporary TRO, there are no statutory requirements (except for those in London mentioned above) on the procedure for making 'special events' orders. Further guidance is, however, given on the Department for Transport's website.

Procedure for making permanent and experimental TRO/TMOs

F23 The procedures for making permanent and experimental TROs/TMOs (that is, including those made under sections 1,6,9, 32 and 45 of the RTRA) are set out in the Local Authorities' Traffic Orders (Procedures) (England and Wales) Regulations 1996.

Consultation

F24 Before making an order, there must be consultation on the proposals as shown in Table F1.

---

200 London Local Authorities Act 1995, section 9

Table F1 Consultation necessary before making an order

Circumstances	Consultee(s)
Where the order relates to, or appears to the order-making authority to be likely to affect traffic on a road for which another authority is the highway authority or the traffic authority	The other authority
Where the order relates to, or appears to the order-making authority to be likely to affect traffic on, a Crown road	The appropriate Crown authority (usually, the Highways Agency)
Where the order relates to, or appears to the order-making authority to be likely to affect traffic on, a road subject to a concession	The concessionaire
Where the order relates to, or appears to the order-making authority to be likely to affect traffic on, a road on which a tramcar or trolley vehicle service is provided	The operator of the service
Where the order relates to, or appears to the order-making authority to be likely to affect traffic on a road outside Greater London which is included in the route of a local service	The operator of the service
Where the order relates to, or appears to the order-making authority to be likely to affect traffic on a road in Greater London which is included in the route of a London bus service	The operator of the service and Transport for London
Where it appears to the authority that the order is likely to affect the passage on any road of ambulances	The chief officer of the appropriate NHS trust
Where it appears to the authority that the order is likely to affect the passage on any road of fire-fighting vehicles	The fire and rescue authority
All cases	(a) The Freight Transport Association (b) The Road Haulage Association (c) Such other organisations (if any) representing persons likely to be affected by any provision in the order as the order-making authority thinks it appropriate to consult

Publicity

F25   Before making a **permanent order**, the traffic authority **must** publicise the proposals by publishing them as follows:

- a notice of intention to make the order in the local press and by such other means it considers appropriate (for example, roadside notices and letters to premises);

- a period of at least 21 days must be allowed for objections to the consultation and notice to be made.

Public inquiry

F26 A traffic authority **must** hold a public inquiry if:

- a bus operator objects to an order that prohibits or restricts the passage of public service vehicles; or
- there is an objection to a prohibition on the loading or unloading of vehicles of any class on any day of the week:
    - at all times;
    - before 07.00 hours;
    - between 10.00 and 16.00 hours; or
    - after 19.00 hours.

F27 A traffic authority may hold a public inquiry in other circumstances.

F28 These publication and objection provisions do not apply to experimental orders. However, an experimental order cannot come into force for at least seven days after a notice of making it has been published. The authority must also comply with the requirements in the procedures regulations for making deposited documents available for public inspection.

Modifications prior to making an order

F29 A traffic authority may modify an order, whether in consequence of any objections or otherwise, before it is made provided the modification does not alter a form already approved by the Secretary of State. If the changes to the order are substantial, the authority **must**[201] carry out further consultation. The authority should:

- tell people likely to be affected by the modifications;
- give them an opportunity of making representations; and
- consider any such representations.

Orders applicable to trunk roads

F30 The procedures are similar in principle to those for orders for other roads and are prescribed in the Secretary of States Traffic Orders (Procedure) (England and Wales) Regulations 1990.

Procedure for making temporary TROs/TMOs

F31 Temporary orders made under section 14 of the Road Traffic Regulation Act 1984 as described above are subject to the Road Traffic (Temporary Restrictions) Procedure Regulations 1992. These are the principal requirements.

- Not less than seven days before making an order, the traffic authority shall publish notice of its intention to make the order in newspaper(s) circulating in the area, and explain its effect.

---

201 S.I. 1996/2489, regulation 14(4)

- The traffic authority shall, on or before the day on which the order is made, give notice:
    - to the Chief Officer of Police of any police area in which any road to which the order relates is situated;
    - where the traffic authority is not the fire authority for the area in which any road to which the order relates is situated, to the chief officer of the fire authority for that area;
    - to any other traffic authority affected by the order; and
    - to any concessionaire directly affected.
- Within 14 days after making the order, the traffic authority shall publish a notice of the making of the order in newspaper(s) circulating in the area.
- When the order has been made but before the instrument comes into force, the traffic authority shall place traffic signs to give road users adequate information as to its effect (and the covering or removal of other signs). Such signs must be maintained as long as the measures are in force.

Review of TRO/TMOs before adoption of CPE powers

F32 The traffic authority should review all existing TRO/TMOs before adopting CPE powers and consider how they should change to meet its parking policy objectives. The review should check whether the restrictions indicated by the signs and road markings are the same as those authorised by the order. The Secretary of State **will not** sign an Order granting CPE until the local authority has confirmed in writing that:

- it has completely reviewed the Traffic Regulation Orders (TROs), traffic signs and road markings within its entire proposed Civil Enforcement Area/Special Enforcement Area in order to highlight any deficiencies;
- it has rectified any deficiencies highlighted as part of this review;
- as a result of this work all TROs, traffic signs and road markings within the entire proposed CEA/SEA conform to the legislation, are consistent with one another and are in a good state of repair; and
- this requirement extends to **all** TROs, traffic signs and road markings with no exceptions and therefore includes existing, new and replacement TROs, traffic signs and road markings.

F33 Parking controls that are not backed by valid TRO/TMOs may be unenforceable and it is likely that any appeals against PCNs will succeed where TRO/TMOs are not valid.

F34 The local authority will need to consider whether restrictions should apply beyond the normal working day and/or at weekends. The authority should examine the scope for relaxing or removing any redundant parking controls. Unnecessary restrictions are very quickly identified when the authority takes over responsibility for their enforcement and this can result in complaints from motorists and bad publicity. It is better to deal with them before civil enforcement commences.

F35 Local authorities may also wish to consider placing all their TRO/TMOs on a graphical information system and on their website so that, for example, they can supply their contractors with accurate, up-to-date maps and inform the public.

Other changes to TRO/TMOs required before taking on CPE power

F36 As part of their review of TRO/TMOs, local authorities should also identify the technical changes which would be needed to comply with the Traffic Management Act 2004. For example, amendments will be needed to reflect the switch from traffic offence provisions to the new system of penalty charges and civil liabilities. Existing on-street and off-street parking orders will need to be amended to reflect the removal of 'initial' and 'excess' parking periods.

F37 If an authority will not removing excess charge flags when introducing CPE, it should include a provision, valid for no more than three months from the introduction of civil parking enforcement, to enable civil enforcement officers to impose a penalty charge when the excess charge flag or display is showing on parking meters (see section below). Similar provision may be needed in off-street car park orders. Once an authority has CPE power, its TRO should not set out the penalty charges, as the Secretary of State sets these.

F38 It would also be expedient for TROs to retain a provision relating to 'anything done with the permission or at the direction of a police constable in uniform' in order to cover emergencies.

F39 Attention is drawn to regulations 21 of The Local Authorities' Traffic Orders (Procedures) (England and Wales) Regulations 1996, which dis-applies most of the normal consultation and making procedures for:

- 'consolidation' orders to re-enact existing provisions without any changes of substance other than those listed in Part 1 of Schedule 4 to the regulations; and
- 'minor' orders in this context, also listed in Schedule 4.

F40 The definition of 'minor' order is not being amended as a consequence of the Traffic Management Act and its subsidiary legislation. This is because TROs/TMOs should not contain matters covered by national legislation.

Parking meters

F41 Local authorities enforcing parking will no longer be using the system of 'initial' and 'excess' parking charges. They will therefore have to remove the 'excess charge' indication from parking meters in CEAs. This change cannot be made overnight, but the Secretary of State believes that all affected meters should be converted within three months of the start of the new penalty charge system in a local authority's area. Meanwhile, an authority should fix notices to unconverted meters stating that it can impose a penalty charge when the excess charge flag or display is showing. These changes will need to be provided for in the relevant TROs.

ANNEX G
SIA guidance on vehicle immobilisation on private land

G1 For the purposes of the following paragraphs, private land is defined as land other than a road within the meaning of the Road Traffic Act 1988.

GI2 Licensing for vehicle immobilisers on private land came into effect across England and Wales on 3 May 2005.

G3 It is now a criminal offence to work as a Vehicle Immobiliser in England and Wales without an SIA licence. If you do work without a licence (or breach the conditions on which your licence was granted) you will be committing a criminal offence, punishable on conviction by a fine of up to £5,000 or six months imprisonment or both.

G4 An exemption to working without a licence is applicable only where the employer or company you work for has been granted Approved Contractor status by the SIA and the other conditions of section 4(4) of the Private Security Industry Act 2001 have also been met. Every condition must be met for this section to apply.

G5 In addition to holding a valid SIA licence and meeting general licence conditions, vehicle immobilisers must observe the following requirements.

1. A vehicle must not be immobilised/ blocked/ towed if:
   - a valid disabled badge is displayed on the vehicle;
   - it is a marked emergency service vehicle which is in use as such.

2. Any licence holder who collects a release fee must provide a receipt, which must include the following:
   - the location where the vehicle was immobilised or towed;
   - their own name and signature;
   - their licence number;
   - the date.

Who needs a licence?

G6 You need a Vehicle Immobiliser's licence if you undertake any of the following:

a. move a vehicle by any means;

b. the restriction of the movement of a vehicle by any means (including the immobilisation of a vehicle by attaching a device to it);

c. the release of a vehicle which has been so moved or restricted, where release is effected by returning the vehicle to the control of the person who was otherwise entitled to remove it, by removing any restriction on the movement of the vehicle by removing the device or by any other means; or

d. the demanding or collecting of a charge as a condition of any such release of or for the removal of the device from a vehicle.

G7 Vehicle immobiliser activity only applies to activities carried out:

- for the purpose of preventing or inhibiting the removal of a vehicle by a person otherwise entitled to remove it;
- where it is proposed to impose a charge for the release of the vehicle;
- in relation to a vehicle while it is elsewhere than on a road within the meaning of the Road Traffic Act 1988.

G8 The requirement to hold a licence when carrying out the immobilisation, restriction or removal activity defined in the Act applies to anyone, e.g. land occupiers, in-house employees, staff supplied for the purposes of or in connection with any contract to a consumer or volunteers.

G9 There are certain exclusions mentioned within the Private Security Industry Act 2001. The Act (paragraphs 2 and 3A of Schedule 2) should be referred to for full details of when a licence is not required.

G10 SIA licensing of vehicle immobilisers does not apply to Scotland.

G11 There are two types of SIA licence:

- A **front line** licence is required if undertaking licensable activity, other than key holding activities (this also covers undertaking non-front line activity). A front line licence is in the form of a credit card-sized plastic card that must be worn, subject to the licence conditions.
- A **non-front line** licence is required for those who manage, supervise and/or employ individuals who engage in licensable activity, as long as front line activity is not carried out – this includes directors* or partners. A non-front line licence is issued in the form of a letter that also covers key holding activities.

For the purposes of the Private Security Industry Act 2001, 'director' means executive and non-executive directors, shadow directors, parent company directors and corporate entities holding a directorship.

Reporting vehicle immobilisers

G12 The SIA welcome any information relating to vehicle immobilisers operating without a licence or in breach of the licensing conditions. This can be reported via the SIA's website at www.the-sia.org.uk.

G13 This information will help the SIA to ensure compliance with the Private Security Industry Act 2001 and thus improve standards in the vehicle immobiliser sector. Please note that the SIA cannot provide feedback on any actions they may take as a result of the information you provide. Please also note that the SIA are unable to pursue cases on behalf of specific individuals.

G14 There are some areas of vehicle immobiliser operations that the SIA do not regulate:

- size of the release fee;
- time taken to release a vehicle;
- adequacy of signage around the site warning that vehicles may be immobilised.

G15 If you feel that you have been treated unfairly you should take this up with the vehicle immobiliser concerned or their employer. If this is not possible or you remain dissatisfied you may wish to consider engaging the services of a solicitor and taking civil legal action. Your local Citizens Advice Bureau or Trading Standards office may be able to offer advice on this.

G16 If a vehicle immobiliser uses threatening behaviour or intimidation they may be committing a criminal offence and the SIA would recommend that you report such instances to the police.

G17 Please note that vehicle immobilising is a legitimate business. If you park on private land without permission you are running the risk of your car being legally clamped, blocked in or towed away.

G18 For more information on vehicle immobilisation on private land visit the SIA website at www.the-sia.org.uk.

ANNEX H
Abbreviations used in this publication

CEA	Civil Enforcement Area
CEO	Civil Enforcement Officer
CPE	Civil Parking Enforcement
CPZ	Controlled Parking Zone
DfT	Department for Transport
DPE	Decriminalised Parking Enforcement
DVLA	Driver and Vehicle Licensing Agency
FCO	Foreign and Commonwealth Office
FPN	Fixed penalty notice
GLA	Greater London Authority
HEB	Health emergency badge
HGV	Heavy goods vehicle
HHC	Hand-held computer
IHIE	Institute of Highway Engineers
LC	London Councils
LIP	Local Implementation Plan
LTP	Local Transport Plan
NoR	Notice of Rejection
NtO	Notice to Owner
PA	Parking Attendant
PCN	Penalty Charge Notice
PPA	Permitted Parking Area
RTRA	Road Traffic Regulation Act 1984
SEA	Special Enforcement Area
SIA	Security Industry Association
SLA	Service Level Agreement
SPA	Special Parking Area
TEC	Traffic Enforcement Centre
TfL	Transport for London
TMA	Traffic Management Act 2004
TMO	Traffic Management Order
TRO	Traffic Regulation Order
VED	Vehicle Excise Duty

Index

abandoned vehicles, 6.14
adjudication, 11.37–11.47, 12.2, 14.3
    Charge Certificates, 10.51
    grounds for appeal, 10.62
    Penalty Charge Notices, 4.17
adjudicators, 10.3, 11.37–11.47
    Civil Enforcement Officers, 6.13
    Codes of Practice, 1.6
advance notice, 5.8–5.9, 5.11–5.13, 8.24
advertising, 5.11
agency agreements, 12.10–12.13
aggressive motorists, 6.21, 8.63
    see also violence
annual reports, 4.16, 4.18, 4.24, 4.28 *see also* reporting
annual returns, PCNs, 4.17
appeals
    allowed, 11.39
    evidence, 8.9, 8.15–8.16
    grounds for, 8.66, 8.70, 11.38
    immobilisation or removal, 8.100
    Notice of Rejection, 11.1, 11.34
    Notice to Owner, 8.40
    Penalty Charge Notices, 4.21
    in progress, 10.61–10.62
    refused, 10.52
    statutory grounds for, 11.44
    time limits, 10.3, 11.38
appraisal
    Civil Parking Enforcement (CPE), 4.1–4.7
    enforcement, 2.11
approved devices, 7.1–7.9, 8.78–8.87
    codes of practice, 8.81–8.82
    detection of contravention, 8.63
    digital cameras, 6.12, 6.21, 8.15–8.16, 8.43
    high speed roads, 13.17
audit trail, 10.4, 11.9
    representations, 11.12, 11.21

back office staff see office staff
bailiffs see certificated bailiffs
benefits, of CPE, 5.14
bicycles see cyclists
Blue Badge Scheme Local Authority Guidance (England), 9.17

Blue badges see disabled badges
borough councils, 12.8
British Parking Association, 1.7, 4.14, 6.3, 11.6, 14.3
bus lanes, 8.83, 12.4
businesses, consultation with, 2.13, 3.3, 8.53–8.54
byelaws, 10.1

cameras *see also* approved devices; digital cameras
    certification of, 8.78
    digital, 6.12, 6.21
    evidence from, 8.15–8.16
cancellation of payment, 8.46, 11.15, 11.29
care workers, 9.36–9.40
casualties, road accidents, 4.21
CCTV, 6.27, 7.5–7.6, 7.8, 8.8
CEA see Civil Enforcement Areas (CEAs)
CEO see Civil Enforcement Officers (CEOs)
certificated bailiffs, 10.64, 10.67–10.68
    terminology change, 10.78
certification, devices of enforcement, 7.1–7.4
challenges see representations, informal
Channel Islands, 10.72
Charge Certificates, 8.20, 10.51–10.54
    county court orders, 10.53
    registration of, 10.55, 10.65
    witness statements, 10.56–10.58
charging consistency, 12.17, 14.10
charging order, 10.74
cheque payments, 10.10, 10.12–10.13, 10.16
Chief Executive Officer, 11.44
City and Guilds qualifications, 6.20
civil debt, 8.20
Civil Enforcement Areas (CEAs), 2.7, 4.25, Annex A
    application procedures, 15.1–15.8
    changes to, 12.9
    levels of enforcement, 13.20
Civil Enforcement of Parking Contraventions (England) General Regulations 2007, 4.24
Civil Enforcement of Parking Contraventions (Guidelines on Levels of Charges) (England) Order 2007, 8.23

Civil Enforcement Officers (CEOs), 2.7,
    6.11–6.17, 8.37, 14.3, Annex D
  CRB checks, 6.10
  dangers to, 6.21, 8.63, 8.66, 13.17
  equipment, 8.2–8.3, 8.14–8.15
  exemptions awareness, 9.43
  identification of, 8.4, 8.7
  immobilisation and removal, 6.13, 8.89,
    8.91–8.93
  performance information, 8.9
  probation period, 6.26
  qualifications for, 6.20
  regulation 10 PCNs, 8.70
  security of, 4.9
  skills and attributes, 6.7–6.9, 6.20
  training, 2.11, 4.4, 6.1, 6.4, 6.18–6.24
  disability awareness, 6.25, 9.14
  transport for, 8.19
  uniforms, 8.4–8.8
Civil Parking Enforcement (CPE), 2.7, 2.9,
    4.1–4.14, 5.14, Annex A
  application for, 12.1–12.2
  HM forces vehicles, 9.33–9.34
  objectives, 3.1–3.4, 3.6–3.9
  powers under, 12.3–12.5
  reporting, 4.15–4.28
Civil Procedure Rules, Part 75, 10.63
clamping see immobilisation
codes of practice, 4.20
  CCTV operation, 6.27, 7.6
  for CEOs, 4.20
  devices of enforcement, 8.81–8.82
  Traffic Enforcement Centre, 10.54
communication, 5.14
  between CEOs, 8.9
  on charging, 14.23, 15.11
  neighbouring authorities, 5.13
  with public, 5.8–5.12, 12.17, 13.4
Communities and Local Government
    Department, 4.29
community councils, 12.17
compassionate grounds, temporary waiving of
    payments, 10.26–10.28
compliance, parking regulations, 4.4, 6.9, 14.8
congestion, 4.21, 9.27, 9.29
consultation, 4.8, 5.1–5.6
  between authorities, 12.9–12.17
  with businesses, 2.13, 3.3, 8.53
  with Civil Enforcement Officers, 3.4, 4.1
  with DVLA, 12.9

  with public, 2.13, 4.3
contractors, 4.7, 4.8, 4.12, 4.23
  costs, 14.3
  immobilisation or removal, 8.91
  informal representations, 11.18
  model contract, 6.3
  registered keeper information, 10.38
contravention codes, 8.23, 8.30–8.34, Annex C
contraventions, 8.9, 8.36–8.47, Annex C
  observation period, 8.48–8.51
Controlled Parking Zones (CPZs), 2.10, 4.4, 5.8
  harmonisation of hours, 12.17
costs of enforcement, 14.3
Council for Tribunals, 15.7
Council of the Isles of Scilly, 12.7
county councils, 12.9–12.13, 15.5
County Court, 10.27
County Surveyors' Society, 1.7
CPE see Civil Parking Enforcement (CPE)
CPZ see Controlled Parking Zones (CPZs)
CRB see Criminal Records Bureau
credit rating, 10.77
criminal activity, 6.14. 13.20
criminal proceedings, 4.9, 10.6
Criminal Records Bureau, 6.10
Crystal Mark guidelines, 5.15
CSS, 1.7
customer service, 4.12
cyclists, 3.3, 8.65

Data Protection Act 1998, 7.5, 7.7
date of service, 11.8
  Notice to Owner, 10.34
  postal PCNs, 8.68, 8.72, 8.87
debt recovery, 8.20, 10.27, 10.64–10.70
Decriminalised Parking Enforcement (DPE), 2.7
  see also Civil Parking Enforcement (CPE)
defective equipment, 6.12
Department for Transport, communication with,
    15.2–15.4
designation orders, 15.1–15.7
devices of enforcement see approved devices
digital cameras, 6.12, 6.21, 8.15–8.17, 8.43
diplomatic immunity, 9.25
Diplomatic Privileges Act 1964, 9.25–9.26
diplomatic vehicles, 6.18, 9.23
  charges required, 9.27–9.29
  recovery, 9.30–9.32
  immobilisation, 8.102, 8.104, 9.25–9.27
  Notices to Owner, 9.30, 10.47

parking tickets, 9.25–9.26
plate types, 9.24
removal, 8.102, 8.104, 9.25–9.26, 9.28–9.29
Disability Discrimination Act 1995, 9.2
Disability Discrimination Act 2005, 9.2
disabled badges
   abuse, 6.13, 9.11–9.19
   Civil Enforcement Officers (CEOs), 9.14
   police involvement, 9.13, 9.16–9.17
   Blue Badge Scheme, 9.4, 9.7, 9.17
   exemptions, 6.21
   gender marker, 9.15
   hazard, 8.103
   holders of, 8.102, 9.5–9.6, 9.9, 9.20–9.22
   immobilisation or removal, 8.102–8.103, 9.9–9.10
   inspection, 6.18, 9.8
   parking concessions, 9.5
   reciprocal arrangements, 9.21
   responsibilities of holders, 9.6–9.7
   withdrawal of, 9.17, 9.18–9.19
disabled people, 3.3, 6.25, 9.2–9.4
   Disabled Persons (Badges for Motor Vehicles) (England) Regulations 2000, 9.17–9.18
discount periods, 8.40, 8.66, 8.70, 8.83, 10.22, 14.16 see also Penalty Charge Notices; penalty charges
   after Notice of Rejection, 11.36
   communication within, 14.16
   informal representations, 11.16
discount rate, penalty charges, 14.19
discretion, 6.16–6.17, 11.4–11.5
   adjudicators, 11.38
dispensations, 9.1, 9.35, 13.21
   care workers, 9.36–9.40
disposal charges, 14.20
Distress for Rent Rules, 10.78
district councils, 12.9–12.13
double parking, 8.57–8.59, 8.60, 12.5
drive aways, 8.63, 8.69–8.75
Driver and Vehicle Licensing Authority (DVLA), 4.8, 4.11
   cooperation with local authorities, 10.45–10.46, 12.2
   information provided from, 10.44–10.46, 12.19
   registered keeper information, 10.38–10.42
   use of personal data, 8.12
dropped footways, 8.57–8.59, 8.61–8.62, 12.5
DVLA see Driver and Vehicle Licensing Authority (DVLA)

e-mail contact, 10.4
earnings order, 10.74
elected members, local authorities, 11.21
emergency services, 8.58, 8.62, 9.42, 12.2
endorsable offences, 4.8, 12.19
enforcement agents, 10.78
enforcement authorities, 1.2, 2.8, 10.1–10.4, 11.4–11.7
   adjudicator's recommendation, 11.44–11.46
   annual return, PCNs, 4.17, 4.30–4.31
   appeals process, 11.39, 11.41–11.43
   choice of measures, 13.16, 13.22–13.24
   costs, 14.2–14.3
   objectives, 3.2–3.4
   payment methods, 10.8–10.10, 10.17–10.20
enforcements, civil court judgments, 10.68
enquiries, from public, 5.10, 6.13
environment, 3.3, 4.20
European disabled badge holders, 9.21
evidence
   approved devices, 8.81
   cases of drive away, 8.70, 8.73
   cases of violence, 8.66
   of contravention, 8.36, 8.43
   digital cameras, 8.15–8.17
   disabled badges, 9.17
   integrity of, 7.5
   Notice to Owner, 10.36
excess charge, 13.10
exemptions, 5.14, 9.1, 9.43, 13.21
   Blue Badge scheme, 6.21
   care workers, 9.36–9.40
   Civil Enforcement Officers, 6.18, 6.22
   emergency vehicles, 8.58, 9.42
   footways and kerbs, 8.58, 8.62
   HM forces vehicles, 9.33–9.34
   loading and unloading, 8.55
   service vehicles, 9.42
   suspension of parking places, 9.41
expenditure, 3.6, 4.24, 14.3–14.4

false representation, 9.17, 11.32
financial information
   annual reports, 4.24
   costs, 14.2–14.4
   expectations of CPE, 3.6–3.9, 13.22, 14.1
   reporting, 4.25–4.29
first class post, 8.66, 8.70, 10.2, 11.8
Fixed Penalty Notices (FPNs), 2.4
forces personnel vehicles, 9.33–9.34

Foreign and Commonwealth Office (FCO), 9.30–9.32
   unpaid PCNs, 10.47
foreign visitors, 10.19, 10.72
   disabled badges, 9.20–9.22
formal representations, 11.18–11.23
FPNs see Fixed Penalty Notices (FPNs)
freight hauliers, 5.4, 6.25
Freight Quality Partnerships, 8.53
Full Guidance on Local Transport Plans, 2.2
Future of Transport White Paper, 2.1

garnishee order, 10.74
grace periods, 8.52
Guidance on Decriminalised Parking Enforcement outside London, 1.5
Guidelines Order, 8.23

hand held computers (HHC), 6.12, 6.21, 8.9–8.13
handbooks, for CEOs, 8.2–8.3
headgear, 8.6
health and safety, 5.4
health care workers see care workers
heavy goods vehicles, 13.13 see also loading and unloading
high speed roads, 12.8, 13.17–13.18
Highway Code, 8.61, 9.6
Highways Agency, 12.2, 13.18–13.19, 15.5
hired vehicles, 10.5, 11.2
HM forces, 9.33–9.34

identification numbers, 6.30, 8.4, 8.7, 8.9, 8.71
immobilisation, 8.88–8.100
   authorisation, 6.13, 6.23
   charges, 14.20
   clamping, 8.96, 9.9
   costs, 14.3
   CPE powers, 12.3
   diplomatic vehicles, 8.102, 8.104, 9.25–9.27
   disabled badges, 8.102–8.103
   fees, vehicle release, 10.18, 10.24, 14.17
   operatives, 6.29–6.30, 8.5, 8.91
   output indicators, 4.12, 4.21
   payment, 8.99, 8.101, 10.24
   private land, 6.29–6.30, 8.5, Annex H
   representations, 11.26, 11.30
   training for, 6.23, 6.28
in-house staff, 4.13
income and expenditure see also revenue
   expectations, 14.3
   penalty charges, 14.17
   recording, 4.25–4.28
   surplus income, 14.7
informal representations, 11.1, 11.10–11.16
Institution of Highways and Transportation, 1.7, 2.18
internal clock, 8.11
internet payments, 10.18, 10.23
Isle of Man, 10.72
IT systems, 10.1, 10.39, 14.3

judicial review, 11.40

kerb space management, 3.3

legal interpretation, 1.3
legal processes, 11.6–11.7, 11.30, 14.3
legal requirement, publication of charges, 14.23
LIP see Local Implementation Plans (LIPs)
loading and unloading, 5.4, 6.21, 8.53–8.56
local Acts, 13.13
local authorities, 2.1–2.2, 2.4–2.5, 12.1, 12.7–12.9
   collaboration, 3.9, 4.10, 5.13, 12.1
   consultation, 12.2, 12.14–12.18, 15.5
   enforcement appraisal, 2.11
   parking policies, 2.10, 2.12, 2.15, 2.18
Local Authorities' Traffic Orders (Procedure) (England and Wales) Regulations 1996, 14.5, 15.8
Local Government Association, Codes of Practice, 1.6
Local Government Technical Advisory Group (TAG), 1.7
Local Implementation Plans (LIPs), 3.4, 4.1
Local Transport Plans (LTPs), 3.4, 4.1
location of vehicle, identification of, 8.42
London see also Local Implementation Plans (LIPs)
   approved devices, 7.1
   Blue Badge Scheme, 9.4
   immobilisation and removal charges, 14.20
   local legislation, 1.1
   parking enforcement, 2.6
   pavement parking, 13.13
   penalty charges, 8.21, 8.23, 8.25, 14.12–14.13
London Councils
   CCTV operation, 7.6
   charges publicity, 8.21
   Codes of Practice, 1.6, 7.6

contravention codes, 8.34
financial reporting, 4.25
London Health Emergency Badge, 9.36
London Technical Advisors Group (LoTAG), 1.7
LoTAG see London Technical Advisors Group
LTP see Local Transport Plans (LTPs)

magistrate court, 9.11
management, staff training, 6.5–6.6
Mayor of London, 1.5, 8.21, 8.25
media, for communication, 5.9, 5.10, 10.4, 11.9
metropolitan district councils, 12.7–12.8
military roads, 12.8
misuse, disabled badges, 9.17
mitigating circumstances, 6.22
mitigation, 6.6
mobile telephones, 8.14
mobility see disabled people
model contracts, 4.14, 6.3
monitoring, 4.15, 14.3 see also reporting
motorcycles, 3.3
motorists, vulnerable, 8.90, 10.26
moving traffic, 4.4, 12.19
multiple PCNs within 24 hours, 8.46

neighbouring authorities, 3.9, 4.10, 5.12, 12.1
Network Management Duty, 3.3
non-payees see persistent evaders
Northampton County Court see Traffic Enforcement Centre (TEC)
Notice of Rejection, 10.50, 11.1, 11.34–11.36
Notice to Owner (NtOs) see also Penalty Charge Notices (PCNs)
  appeals, 8.20, 8.40
  cancellation of, 11.29
  corporate bodies, 10.43
  diplomatic vehicles, 9.30, 10.47
  limitation period, 10.11, 10.32
  must state, 10.33
  not received, 10.58–10.59
  payment cancelled, 10.37
  Penalty Charge Notices, 8.63, 8.66, 8.70, 8.84, 10.35
  purpose, 10.32
  registered keeper information, 10.38–10.42
  representations, 6.16, 10.33, 10.36, 11.1
  service of, 10.34, 10.35, 11.8
notices see Notice of Rejection; Notice to Owner; Penalty Charge Notices
NtO see Notice to Owner

NVQs, parking control, 6.20
objectives
  Operational Guidance, 1.2
  parking policy, 13.22
observation periods, 8.48–8.52, 8.77
occupancy rates, 14.9
off-street parking, 4.25, 12.12
Office of the Chief Executive, 11.44
office staff
  consultation with, 3.4, 4.1
  discretion, 6.16
  skills and training, 6.2, 6.5–6.6
older people, 9.3
on-street parking, 2.4, 14.9
  district councils, 12.9–12.13
  income reporting, 4.25
online payment, 10.8, 10.17
oral examination, debt recovery, 10.73
out-of-hours payment facilities, 10.25
outcome indicators, 4.12
owner of vehicle see also Notices to Owner (NtOs)
  consent not given, 11.23
  not registered with DVLA, 8.88, 8.105
  Penalty Charge Notice, 8.63, 8.74
  recent change, 11.23, 11.29
  registered keeper, 10.38–10.43
  untraceable, 10.44–10.45

parish councils, 12.17
parking account, 4.24
parking adjudicators see adjudicators
parking attendants (PAs), 2.7, 6.14 see also Civil Enforcement Officers (CEOs)
parking charges, 14.5–14.10
parking concessions, disabled badges, 9.5
parking meters, 6.13, 13.10
parking policies, 2.2–2.3, 2.10, 2.15, 2.18, 3.3
  appraisal of, 4.1–4.9, 13.1–13.3, 13.14
  awareness of, 5.7–5.13
  contravention of more than 1 restriction, 8.45
  cost-effectiveness, 12.13
  enforcement regime, 13.5, 13.16, 13.22–13.24
parking vouchers, 6.14
part payment, 10.8, 10.27–10.28
pavements
  dropped, 8.57–8.58, 8.61–8.62, 12.5
  parking on, 13.13–13.15
pay and display machines, 6.13
payment

centres, 10.8, 10.23–10.24
discount periods, 10.22
incorrect, 10.12–10.15
late, 10.21
methods, 8.100, 10.8–10.10, 10.16–10.18, 10.23
Notice to Owner limitation period, 10.11
paid, 10.20
part payment, 10.8, 10.27
for release of vehicle, 10.28, 10.30
subject to conditions, 10.14
temporary waiving of, 10.26–10.28
PCN see Penalty Charge Notices (PCNs)
pedestrian crossings, 10.6, 11.23, 12.20
pedestrians, 3.3, 13.20
Penalty Charge Notices (PCNs), 2.5, 3.6, 4.24, 11.3, 14.3
annual returns on, 4.17, 4.30–4.31
approved devices, 8.78, 8.81, 8.84–8.86
cancellation, 11.4, 12.20
contraventions, 6.21, 8.37, 8.45–8.46
copies of, 8.39
criminal activity, 12.20
fixed to vehicle, 8.37
hand held computers, 8.9, 8.39
identification of, 8.26–8.28
immobilisation or removal following, 8.92
income from, 4.25
information contained
additional, 8.44
essential, 8.40, 8.66, 8.70, 8.84
recommended, 8.41, 8.67, 8.71, 8.85–8.86
not issued, 6.17, 8.35
as Notice to Owner, 8.63, 8.66, 8.70, 8.84, 10.35
paid, 10.20
prevention of service, 6.21
regulations 9 and 10, 8.40, 8.66, 8.70, 8.75, 11.2
representations against, 6.9, 11.1–11.2
return of owner, 8.76–8.77
serving of, 6.12, 8.77, 8.80
by post, 8.37, 8.63–8.67
two or more within 24 hours, 8.46
unenforceable, 6.13, 8.35
uniform of officer, 8.5, 8.6
unique numbers, 8.26–8.29
written by hand, 8.9, 8.39
penalty charges, 3.8, 14.12, 14.15–14.17
bands, 2.11, 14.11, 14.13
changes to, 8.24, 14.25
criminal proceedings, 10.6
levels, 4.4, 8.22, 8.23
London, 8.21, 8.25, 14.12–14.13
payable by owner, 8.20, 10.5
payment, 8.40, 8.47, 10.8–10.10, 10.18
surcharge, 14.17
VAT, 14.24
performance measures
authorities, 4.18, 4.22
parking enforcement policies, 4.21–4.22, 4.24
quality of service, 10.2
staff, 4.12
performance targets, 3.6, 4.21–4.23, 8.99, 10.2
Permitted Parking Area (PPA), 2.7 see also Civil Enforcement Areas (CEAs)
persistent evaders, 8.92, 8.96, 8.105–8.107, 12.3
definition of, 8.105
diplomatic vehicles, 9.27
personal identity see disabled badges; identification numbers
photo-identity cards, 8.7
picking up and setting down, 6.21
plain English, 5.15
planning policies
loading and unloading, 8.54
parking, 2.14–2.15
Planning Policy Guidance 13, 2.15–2.18
Planning Policy Statement 3, 2.15, 2.17
pocket books, 6.21
police
consultation with, 4.3, 4.8–4.9, 12.21, 15.5
notification of vehicles removed, 8.98, 8.103
parking enforcement, 2.1, 2.4–2.5
Civil Enforcement Areas, 12.19–12.20
trunk roads, 13.18
removal, Blue Badge vehicle, 9.10
traffic offences responsibilities, 4.9
vehicle not registered, 8.105
postage
delays in, 10.21
first class, 8.66, 8.70, 10.2, 11.8
power to inspect legislation, 9.16
PPG13, 2.15–2.18
PPS3, 2.15, 2.17
prescribed functions, 8.4
pricing, of parking, 4.4
privacy, 7.5
private land, immobilisation on, 6.29–6.30
Private Security Industry Act 2001, 6.29
procedural impropriety, 11.23

processes and procedures, 1.2, 2.8, 10.1
promissory notes, 10.26
public interest, 11.4, 12.13, 13.22
public perception, 8.1, 8.78, 8.90, 13.4
   appeals process, 11.42
public services, 4.20
   understanding of, 5.1, 5.7, 5.10
public transport, 3.3, 4.21, 13.22, 14.8
publication, of charges, 14.23, 14.25, 15.11
   see also communication, with public

qualifications, 6.20, 6.27
quality assurance, 10.1
quality of service, 10.1–10.4

R v. LB Camden (ex parte Cran), 3.7
recovery, of vehicle, 8.99
registered keeper (see also owner of vehicle), 10.38–10.43
registration, Charge Certificate, 10.55, 10.65
Regulation of Investigatory Powers Act 2000 (RIPA), 9.11
regulations, precedence of, 1.3
regulations 9 and 10 PCN see Penalty Charge Notices
relevant date, 10.32
removal of vehicle, 8.89–8.90, 8.99–8.101, 9.9–9.10
   authorisation, 6.13, 6.23
   charges, 14.20
   costs, 14.3
   CPE powers, 12.3
   diplomatic vehicles, 9.25–9.26, 9.28–9.29
   disposal charges, 9.29, 10.28
   fees, 10.18, 10.24, 14.17
   hazard or obstruction, 8.88, 8.95, 9.9
   operatives, 6.28–6.29, 8.5, 8.91
   payment centres, 10.23–10.25
   persistent evaders, 8.106
   photograph of vehicle, 8.17
   representations, 11.27, 11.30
   return of driver, 8.96
   sale proceeds, 11.30
   where parking is permitted, 8.92
reporting, 4.15–4.24
   financial, 4.25–4.29
representations
   advice on rights, 10.30–10.31, 11.15
   consideration of, 11.28–11.31
   contracting out, 11.18
   decisions, 11.28, 11.31, 11.33
   delayed, 11.24
   discretion, 11.4–11.5, 11.24
   effective processes, 11.20
   false, 9.17, 11.32
   formal, 11.18–11.24
   grounds for, 8.66, 10.30, 11.22, 11.26
   immobilisation or removal, 8.100, 11.25–11.27
   informal, 11.10–11.17
   procedures for, 8.76
   rejection of, 10.50, 11.1, 11.34–11.36
   separation of duties, 11.19
   statutory grounds for, 10.36
   time limits, 8.66, 8.70, 8.84, 8.100, 10.33
residents, parking policies, 2.17
   permits, 8.78
revenue, 4.24, 6.15
   benefits from, 4.15
   raising of, 3.6–3.9
road markings see traffic signs
road safety, 3.3
Road Traffic Act 1988, 13.13
Road Traffic Act 1991 (RTA), 1.1–1.2, 2.4–2.5, Annex B
Road Traffic Regulation Act 1984 (RTRA), 1.5
   disabled badge abuse, 9.17
   parking charges, 14.5
   parking policies, 2.4
   s. 55, 3.8, 4.24, 4.25, 6.15, 14.7
   s. 63A, 6.14
   surplus income, use of, 4.27
   Traffic Regulation Orders (TROs), 4.5, 13.14
road user groups, 4.8
RTRA see Road Traffic Regulation Act 1984

Scotland, 10.72
Security Industry Association (SIA), 6.29, Annex G
security issues, 12.19
self-financing enforcement, 3.9
service level agreements (SLAs), 4.13–4.14
service vehicles, 8.58, 9.42
setting down, 6.21
signing see traffic signs
SLA see Service Level Agreements (SLAs)
social inclusion, 11.9
sole traders, 10.43
Special Enforcement Areas (SEAs), 8.58, 12.6, Annex A

Special Parking Areas (SPAs), 2.7 see also Civil Enforcement Areas (CEAs)
stakeholders, 5.2
stationary vehicles, 6.14
statistical information, 4.24, 8.30
statutory declaration see witness statements, Charge Certificates
statutory duties, 1.3, 15.5
statutory grounds for appeal, 11.44
Statutory Guidance, 1.3–1.4
Statutory Instruments, 1.5
statutory period, payments, 10.21
statutory representations, 11.10
storage charges, 8.101, 14.20
supervisors, training of, 6.4, 6.6
surcharge, 8.66, 8.70, 8.84, 10.48, 14.17
    see also Charge Certificates
surveys, on-street enforcement, 6.14
suspension of parking places, 6.14, 8.18, 9.41
sustainable transport, 2.15

TAG see Local Government Technical Advisory Group
targets, 8.99, 10.2
tax discs see Vehicle Excise Duty (VED)
TEC see Traffic Enforcement Centre (TEC)
telephone contact, 10.4
    payments, 8.100, 10.8, 10.21
time limits
    adjudicator's recommendation accepted, 11.47
    appeals, 11.38
    correspondence, 10.3
    decision notices, 11.28
    enforcement authorities, 11.45
    payment, 8.40
    quality of service, 10.2
    representations, 8.66, 8.70, 8.84, 8.100, 11.28
    warrants of execution, 10.69
TMA see Traffic Management Act 2004
town councils, 12.17
TRACE, 8.98, 8.103
Traffic Enforcement Centre (TEC), 4.8, 8.27, 8.29
    county court orders, 10.54
    local authority consultation, 12.2
    recovery of charge, 10.53
    transfer to County Court, 10.76
    warrants of execution, 10.64
traffic flow, 4.4, 12.19
traffic management, 4.21, 8.88
    appraisal of, 13.1–13.3

Traffic Management Act 2004 (TMA)
    approved devices, certification, 8.78
    Blue Badge Scheme, 9.8, 9.16
    diplomatic immunity, 9.26
    double parking and dropped footways, 8.58
    management of road network, 2.1
    Network Management Duty, 3.3
    on-street parking account, 4.26
    parking on trunk roads, 13.18
    Part 6, 1.1–1.2, 1.5, 2.6, 12.4
    persistent evaders, 8.106
    purpose of, 6.14
    representations against PCNs, 6.9
    s. 87, 1.3–1.4
    s. 90, 9.33
    Sch. 7, 4.25
    Traffic Regulation Orders, 13.10
    warrant of execution, 10.69
Traffic Management Orders (TMOs) see Traffic Regulation Orders
traffic orders see Traffic Regulation Orders
Traffic Regulation Orders (TROs), 2.3, 13.6–13.12
    amendments for CPE, 13.10, 15.8
    emergencies, 13.11
    exemptions under, 8.54, 9.42
    invalid, 11.23
    mapping of, 13.9
    review of, 2.10, 2.12, 4.4–4.5, 12.1, 13.6, 15.8, Annex F
    timing of restrictions, 13.8
traffic signs, 2.10, 4.4, 12.7
    appropriate, 8.63, Annex E
    defective, 6.13, 8.35
    pavement parking, 13.13
Traffic Signs Regulations 2002, 12.17
traffic wardens see Civil Enforcement Officers (CEOs)
training, 2.11, 4.4, 11.6
    Civil Enforcement Officers (CEOs), 6.1, 6.4, 6.18–6.25
    costs, 14.3
    devices of enforcement, 8.81
    disability awareness, 9.14
    immobilisation or removal, 8.91
    importance of, 6.1, 6.3
Transport Act 2000, 12.4
Transport for London, 8.21, 8.25, 14.12, 14.14
Tribunals, Courts and Enforcement Act 2007, 10.78
Tribunals for Users programme, 11.41

TRO *see* Traffic Regulation Orders (TROs)
trunk roads, 13.17–13.18
undertakers' vehicles, 13.22
uniforms, 6.30, 8.4–8.8
unitary authorities, 12.7–12.8
unloading *see* loading and unloading
untraceable owners, 10.44–10.45
utility companies, complaints from, 14.10

VAT issues, 14.24
VED *see* Vehicle Excise Duty (VED)
Vehicle Certification Agency (VCA), 7.1, 7.4
Vehicle Excise and Registration Act 1994, 9.34
Vehicle Excise Duty (VED), 4.11, 6.14, 10.46
vehicle registration system, 6.21
vehicles, identification of, 8.9
verbal warnings, 6.21
Vienna Convention on Diplomatic Relations, 9.25–9.26

violence, against CEO, 8.63, 8.65
    Penalty Charge Notice by post, 8.66–8.68
vulnerable people, 8.90, 10.26

waivers, 9.1, 9.35, 13.21 *see also* dispensations
warning notices, 6.13, 14.24
warrants of control, 10.78
warrants of execution, 10.64–10.76
website, use of, 5.11
wheel clamping *see* immobilisation
White Paper on Diplomatic Immunities and Privileges, 9.25 *see also* diplomatic vehicles
width, of road, 13.14
witness statements, 6.13
   cases of violence, 8.66
   Charge Certificates, 10.56–10.58, 10.63
working day, 8.68
written by hand, PCNs, 8.9, 8.39

Printed in the United Kingdom by TSO
N5808715 05/08